MAR - - 2003

The Man Who Changed How Boys and Toys Were Made

The Man Who Changed How Boys and Toys Were Made

Bruce Watson

VIKING

VIKING
Published by the Penguin Group
Penguin Putnam Inc., 375 Hudson Street,
New York, New York 10014, U.S.A.
Penguin Books Ltd, 80 Strand,
London WC2R 0RL, England
Penguin Books Australia Ltd, 250 Camberwell Road, Camberwell,
Victoria 3124, Australia
Penguin Books Canada Ltd, 10 Alcorn Avenue,
Toronto, Ontario, Canada M4V 3B2
Penguin Books India (P) Ltd, 11 Community Centre, Panchsheel Park,
New Delhi–110 017, India
Penguin Books (N.Z.) Ltd, Cnr Rosedale and Airborne Roads,
Albany, Auckland, New Zealand
Penguin Books (South Africa) (Pty) Ltd, 24 Sturdee Avenue,
Rosebank, Johannesburg 2196, South Africa

Penguin Books Ltd, Registered Offices:
Harmondsworth, Middlesex, England

First published in 2002 by Viking Penguin,
a member of Penguin Putnam Inc.

1 3 5 7 9 10 8 6 4 2

Erector is a trademark of Meccano SN.
This book is not endorsed or authorized by this company.

Grateful acknowledgment is made for permission to reprint "Magic" from *Where the Sidewalk Ends* by Shel Silverstein. Copyright © 1974 by Evil Eye Music, Inc. Used by permission of HarperCollins Publishers.

CIP data available

ISBN 0-670-03134-8

This book is printed on acid-free paper. ∞

Printed in the United States of America
Set in Stempel Garamond
Designed by Jaye Zimet

To my mother, who taught this boy to build with words, and to my wife, who encourages this man to play with them for a living

Contents

Prologue

In the fall of 1961, the world was coming apart. The Berlin Wall had been built that August, and by October, Russian and American tanks squared off one hundred yards apart at Checkpoint Charlie. The two superpowers had resumed nuclear testing, making thinly veiled threats about their nuclear muscle and sending explicit messages in megatons. The Soviet Union unleashed a terrifying sixty-megaton bomb above the Russian steppe. In a nationally televised speech, President Kennedy urged Americans to build their own fallout shelters, and *Life* soon whipped up the frenzy with a cover story. Panicked, some 200,000 families built shelters and stockpiled supplies for the coming Armageddon. Elsewhere, there were crises in the Congo, in Laos, and in a festering sore called Vietnam. Across Africa and Asia, tired old empires were dying while sanguine new countries were struggling to be born.

In those days before around-the-clock news, fear filtered slowly into elementary schools. I knew no more about the world's unraveling than what I learned in third grade. Our teacher, Mrs. Williams, a short, blond woman with a pleasingly plump face, assured us we would be safe. We were thirty miles from L.A., she said again and again. The worst an atomic bomb might do was blow in our classroom windows. That's why we had to lower the blinds—to block any flying glass—before we ducked and covered under our desks. But I had little time to care about things falling apart. I was too busy putting things together with the gift I had received for my eighth birthday—an Erector set.

It was the heaviest of all the packages I found on the dining room table. It was the only one that rewarded me for shaking it— clanking like some steel robot in a cage. When I emptied the set on our linoleum floor, pure possibility spread before me. Shiny girders, notched along their length, clattered against each other. Each seemed to invite the tiny nuts and bolts that came in a separate package. Perforated steel plates promised to be the flatbed of any truck or the road crossing any bridge I cared to build. There were bright brass wheels notched around each rim to double as pulleys. There were miniature crankshafts, six-inch axles, and yellow and red steel plates in odd assorted shapes. The set came with a manual, but like all manuals, it wasn't much good. It pictured dozens of models but offered no instructions whatsoever. Merely by studying the drawings, I was supposed to whip together a Walking Beam Engine, a Gantry Crane, or a Grocery Wagon. I tossed the manual aside. I was eight now. I'd build what I *wanted* to build. Besides, what was a Gantry Crane, anyway?

Within days of opening my Erector set, I had made several metal mutants. Dutifully, I cranked out a simple slide, a small wagon, and a crane that looked more like those found in wetlands than on a construction site. Only then did I look at the manual. On the inside cover I found "A Personal Message from the Inventor of Erector." I was "a lucky boy to get an Erector Set," the message said. "No other construction set contains so many different parts and builds so many different models." Did I know that the U.S. Patent Office had issued more than one hundred patents for Erector parts? I sure didn't. But I was about to learn that Erector provided "double-header fun" because "every new model will bring you a new thrill." The message was signed,

"Your friend, A. C. Gilbert." And there on the inside cover was a black-and-white picture of the "inventor of Erector and founder of the Gilbert Hall of Science."

Slightly balding with a hint of a sneer, A. C. Gilbert didn't look like anyone's friend. He looked more like some physics professor in dire need of a sabbatical. I found it hard to believe he had invented the Erector set, or that anyone had. This pile of girders, nuts, and bolts couldn't be an "invention" like our TV or hi-fi. Instead it seemed like a replica of the industrial world, as if the steel girders of local buildings in progress had been re-created in miniature. The Erector set couldn't have been "invented." It just *was*.

Throughout that fall, while the world unraveled, I struggled to assemble a world of my own. I managed to build a simple Sled and a miniature bridge. One rainy weekend, I even built the Farm Wagon. While the rain drummed on my bedroom window, my wagon rolled across the floor. After several days of rolling, I parked it on a shelf for the winter. But for every model I finished, I trashed two or three. Frustrated by screws the size of ants, I hurled my Windmill Pump across the bedroom. Furious at girders that would not fit where I needed them, I twisted my See Saw Wagon until it could neither see nor saw. Finally, after months of wrestling with it, I put my Erector set in the closet and only took it out on rainy days. I had other toys to play with by then. Robots that talked. Police cars with real sirens. Walkie-talkies. Silly Putty.

I soon forgot all about my Erector set. Its pieces were scattered and left to rust who knows where. The simple steel toy that helped me assemble a world no longer seemed a part of my childhood, nor of anyone else's. In college, when talk turned to beloved toys, we boomers shared fond memories of hula hoops and Etch A Sketches. Erector sets? No one I knew ever mentioned one. But years later I learned that I had been asking the wrong kids. And I was just as wrong about A. C. Gilbert, the ersatz college professor who claimed to be my "friend." To me he was just a casual acquaintance, but he had once been the best friend boys and the toy industry ever had.

A. C. Gilbert made more than toys. He manufactured future engineers and scientists. For fifty years, toys made by the A. C. Gilbert Company stood above the crowd of cheap doodads and gewgaws peddled to make a quick buck. Gilbert himself— athlete, magician, toy tycoon, radio pioneer—was an assemblage of diverse parts. An American original, he was part Horatio Alger, part Jim Thorpe, and part P. T. Barnum. Conservative and straitlaced, he nonetheless embraced the most progressive views on education. In an age when learning was by rote, Gilbert encouraged children to make up their education as they went along. He knew kids learned this way because he had been a boy in the truest sense, in our truest, bluest era.

Growing up in the 1890s, Gilbert came of age in a time almost devoid of irony or cynicism. Concepts such as honor, duty, and success were touted in public on a daily basis, and except for Mark Twain, few dared snigger or scoff. Terms like "plucky" and "alert" were applied to boys like Gilbert without the slightest sarcasm. Pride was still pride, and heroes were not yet doomed to be toppled from their pedestals by scandal or skeletons in closets. Stiffened by such moral fiber, Gilbert drove himself to become a mass of muscle in a slight frame. From 1900 to 1910 he was America's greatest amateur athlete. A national champion collegiate wrestler, he also won sprints and hurdles, quarterbacked a college football team, and set world records in the pole vault. But although he had devoutly followed the Protestant work ethic, Gilbert then thumbed his nose at it.

In 1909, shelving his M.D. from Yale University, Gilbert chose to practice boyhood instead of medicine. While others went to work, he made a living by making and selling magic tricks. Two years later, he invented the Erector set. It was an instant success, allowing him to remain a boy in a businessman's body. Throughout his life, he had a childlike delight in fun tempered by a business sense that made him a millionaire back when that term was still gilded. While other toy makers were content to surrender their toys to the market's whims, Gilbert created the modern toy industry by selling fun all year round. He promoted his products with a dizzying array of contests, monthly magazines, and engineering "institutes." In sprawling full-page magazine ads filled with a homespun paternalism, Gilbert spoke to boys as if they were his friends. And they wrote back, sending him some 300,000 letters a year, many of them signed "your loving son."

Between 1913 and 1966, Gilbert sold more than 30 million Erector sets, earning its nickname as "the world's greatest toy." But it's hard to consider it a toy. During the late 1920s the top-of-the-line Erector set, packed in a wooden box two and a half feet square and eight inches thick, weighed 150 pounds and made hundreds of models, including a five-foot-long zeppelin and a four-foot Hudson steam locomotive. The set sold for $70, a month's wages during the Great Depression. But along with Erector sets, A. C. Gilbert made science in a box. He manufactured weather kits, astronomy kits, chemistry sets, microscopes, telescopes, and mini-labs that let kids play with physics, hydraulic engineering, mineralogy, sound, light, telegraphy, civil engineering, magnetism, even atomic energy. Gilbert's toys allowed boys (and any girls who could get their brothers' permission) to apprentice at an early age, trying on the world of science and industry to see how it fit. But above all, A. C. Gilbert made memories. Too many of these have passed on with their owners, but some still cause adults to behave rather strangely in their wake.

On a rainy summer Saturday, nearly forty years after I got my Erector set, I am standing outside a factory on a shady street in New Haven, Connecticut. I don't often tour old factories and can't imagine why anyone would. Upon learning about the tour of Erector Square, I expected perhaps a dozen people to show up.

I knew that Erector sets had become collectibles in the 1980s, along with baseball cards, Pez dispensers, and anything else that smacked of Boomer nostalgia. (A top-of-the-line Erector set from the 1920s can sell for $15,000.) Along with paying such prices, collectors will go to absurd lengths to get additional pieces that pertain to their collections. Still, I couldn't imagine anyone shelling out $40 to tour an empty factory. Yet when I enter the waiting room, more than a hundred men and women have come out in the rain to learn more about Alfred Carleton Gilbert and his work. An adjacent room is filled with displays—Erector set ads, a whirling Erector Ferris Wheel, a few old sets perfectly preserved in wooden boxes. All around them, people shuffle along, talking low-tech.

"This was the Number Eight, the one that built the zeppelin."

"I had that model over there, but without the motor. I remember on Christmas my dad and uncle played with it for about an hour before I got a chance."

"Check out that Ferris Wheel!"

After a few minutes, a tour guide divides us into two groups. I leap into the first and am soon outside in a light drizzle, looking up at Erector Square. The three-story brick building looks like the backdrop for a Mafia movie. Some walls are covered in ivy; others bear faded lettering from stenciled signs. In recent years, our guide says, the building has been converted to studios and offices. Dozens of artists work here, along with a graphic design firm, a yoga practice, a chiropractor, and a masseuse. But the building still has the same name, "and not a week goes by where we don't get a letter or a call from someone who remembers Mr. Gilbert."

Our tour group is an eclectic bunch. Men in their fifties or sixties wear baseball caps with train logos. Some insignias recall real trains—Santa Fe or Union Pacific. Another, American Flyer, was the toy train line Gilbert bought in 1938. Gray-haired women beneath umbrellas clutch at each other's elbows as they tread the slippery sidewalk. One young man carries a cell phone, but the rest have the look of aging hobbyists, people more comfortable behind a model railroad layout than in a crowd. Yet as they get to know each other, they find they have much in common. Some worked for A. C. Gilbert. "He was a wonderful man," a bent old woman remembers out loud. "If it was your birthday, he'd come up to you, shake your hand, kiss you on the cheek. Even if you were on the night shift. We didn't have a union, you know. We voted against it because Mr. Gilbert treated us so well." Others know Gilbert secondhand, but they know everything about him. As we move into an open courtyard, the group exchanges "Did you knows?" that sound as if they came from my Erector set manual.

"Did you know that Mr. Gilbert set the world record for the pole vault?"

"Did you know that he won the Olympics in 1908?"

"Did you know that Mr. Gilbert once saved Christmas?" That I certainly did not know. I wait to hear how he performed this Grinch-defying feat, but as we circle the plant looking for an open door, the story dissolves into other Gilbert anecdotes. How Mr. Gilbert ran Connecticut's first radio station. How he owned a 600-acre estate he called Paradise. How he hired a circus car and sent it around the country pitching his toys. Just when I suspect I have heard the entirety of the man's life, we find an entrance at the rear of the factory and duck in out of the rain. Finally, we get to *see* something. Our first stop—the Erector Square power plant. Only a group raised with a nuts-and-bolts sense of how things work could marvel at this visit to a labyrinth of pipes, valves, and gauges.

"Look at those pipes!"

"And dials. These days, that whole panel would be a digital readout." Then we climb steps, our presence echoing through the brick stairway. At the top of three cramped flights, we reach a walnut-paneled office overlooking the courtyard. The word spreads through the crowd. This was "*his* office." Cameras come out of tote bags. People take photos of each other standing before

Mr. Gilbert's fireplace or in the corner where Mr. Gilbert's desk stood. Someone asks where Mr. Gilbert kept his chinning bar. "Did you know he held the world record for chin-ups? And even when he was in his fifties, he used to chin himself at work."

After an hour, the tour concludes. The second group is waiting its turn. As we descend the stairs, the crowd's enthusiasm suggests that I've missed out on a piece of the puzzle called American childhood. When I got my Erector set in 1961, it already seemed dated, but for those a generation older, A. C. Gilbert's toys were an integral part of growing up. In this one toy they found a model that still shapes the way they view work, industry, and America. I find myself wondering whatever happened to Erector sets. I ask myself why my children's toys bear so little relation to reality. Fantasy has always been an integral part of play, but have modern children, hurried toward adulthood, begun to cling to it a little too long? Have adults decided that the modern world, with its manic pace and bewildering technology, is not fit to model for children? Or is it just toys that seem dumber, more sinister, and totally at odds with the world around them?

Time changes the way we build and design. Brick and stone surrender to fiberglass. Pencil and paper become silicon chips. Dials and meters morph into digital readouts. Yet an industrial way of thinking survives in the computer age. It lives on in the basements of Silicon Valley offices, where janitors keep the heat going. It thrives in kitchens where a recipe for cornbread is still found in a cookbook, not on a Web site. It is housed in garages with walls lined from floor to rafters in tools. And no matter how many Nintendo or Sega systems are sold this year, there remains a gang of older kids who remember simpler toys. They recall the days when batteries were not included because they were not needed. They remember a Christmas morning when time stood still just long enough for a single gift, a gift that turned out to be not a sweater or jacket but a toy, the one that topped the wish list.

Toys are not merely what we play with. If we lend them our

youth, piling out of bed in the morning to get our hands on them again, they construct a kingdom in our minds. That kingdom lasts as long as we do. Today's most popular toys—even those for thirteen-year-olds—are pure fantasy. But time was when toys were mock-ups of the grown-up world, preparing children for it day by day, doll by doll, model by model. When a society is in sync with its toys, children are not afraid to grow up, and those who come of age with such toys can look back and see the person they've become in the toys they once loved. If, as William Wordsworth said, "the Child is father of the Man," then the right toy is one of many mothers. I was amazed that one hundred people showed up to tour an abandoned toy factory. But the crowd has made me realize how much toys matter, and how a visionary like A. C. Gilbert can shape generations. How many thousands might have come here had they known that Erector Square was still around?

As we step back into the courtyard, I notice some railroad tracks behind the factory. These are the tracks that used to carry Erector sets to market. With their Y-shaped switches and parallel rails, the tracks remind me of the HO train set I once had. My set had electricity flowing through the tracks, but this railroad is electrified from above. A lattice of power lines and rusted steel girders bridges the rails. Each piece of steel is notched, form fitted, and bolted in place. And for a moment, I can imagine a lean, athletic man fresh out of Yale riding along these tracks toward Manhattan. It's a half century before the world began to come apart. In the fall of 1911, toys are luxuries, their purchase saved for the holidays, their purpose mere diversion. But A. C. Gilbert, his head then full of hair, his eyes narrowed with determination to play *and* succeed, looks out the window. He sees the girders overhead. He wonders.

> *There was a child went forth every day*
> *And the first object that he look'd upon, that object he became.*
> —WALT WHITMAN

1

Something Up His Sleeve

Running about a decade late, but eager to catch up, the New York, New Haven & Hartford Railroad was joining the century of progress in the fall of 1911. Beyond the tracks, the era bustled with adventure and industry. That summer, Hiram Bingham had trekked out of New Haven and into the Andes to discover Machu Picchu, the lost city of the Incas. Farther south, on the edge of Antarctica, Roald Amundsen and Robert Scott hunkered down in the frozen darkness, readying for their race to the South Pole. And on the sidewalks of New York, huddled masses of immigrants, having just taken the greatest leap of their lives, spoke of "a new Renaissance." The America of 1911 was a hustling place, sprouting tall buildings, taming its trusts, and striding into the world arena in new outposts from Panama to the Philippines. That fall, late but eager to catch up, the New York, New Haven & Hartford Railroad joined the century of progress by switching from steam power to electricity.

Tracks were lined with cranes and girders as workmen built a power grid from Manhattan toward New Haven. Along with Connecticut's fall foliage of yellow birch and red maple, construction became the railroad's sideshow. Instead of viewing the grimy backsides of Stamford and Bridgeport, passengers could chart progress in steel. By some given Monday, workers had extended the electrification towers to a certain rusty chain-link fence or a backyard with a clothesline and BVDs flapping in the wind. By Wednesday, the construction had gone beyond the fence or backyard, reaching another landmark. That pile of steel on the ground Thursday morning—would it be a tower by Friday afternoon? Looking out train windows, dozens watched, yet only one wondered. Wondered whether boys like him would enjoy building with their own girders.

Boys like him, as if there were many. As he rode the train to Manhattan, A. C. Gilbert was twenty-seven going on seven. He wore the commuter's uniform—a suit, tie, and a face as blank as a new ledger sheet. He was smaller than average—five foot seven, 135 pounds—yet he carried himself with the assurance of a much larger man. His hair was the color of corroded steel. Above his triangular torso he had jug-handle ears and large brown eyes that stared through any camera. In contemporary slang, he was a "go-getter," having passed all the masculine tests of his time. He had a degree in medicine from Yale and a long list of world-class athletic achievements. Yet anyone on the train who chose to speak with him would have found him humble, quiet, even a bit dull. When he used the past tense, he dwelt in platitudes—"That was the biggest day of my life," "It was the most exciting thing that ever happened to me." When he spoke of the future, he was boyishly upbeat, as if there would be no politics, no recessions, no wars to slow his steady ascent. But he rarely mentioned his business, his medals, or his records. Only the small New Haven apartment he shared with a wife and a daughter displayed his success. There on shelves sat hundreds of trophies, certificates, plaques, congratulatory telegrams, news clippings, and a photo of him receiving an Olympic gold medal. And scattered throughout the apartment were the magic tricks he was always inventing or improving to make his living. Gilbert had earned the three-piece suit of manhood, yet he wore it like a pair of knickers. Inside it remained the raw energy of a restless boy on his way to Manhattan to perform magic in a storefront window.

As he sat on the train, Gilbert kept one hand on his sample case, the other at his side. The hidden hand anxiously turned over a coin, rolling it across knuckles, backpalming it to send it up a sleeve. Since winning a magic kit as a boy, Gilbert had been steadily honing his sleight of hand. Whether in class, studying, or courting his future wife, he had kept that one hand in the realm of illusion. Friends laughed at how often he dropped a half-dollar in the middle of a lecture, meal, or conversation, yet constant practice had made Gilbert a first-rate magician. Since coming to New Haven in 1905, he had risen from $5 performances at children's parties to $100-a-night shows in clubs throughout Connecticut and New York. One such show billed him as "GILBERT, assisted by Madame Darsone and Will Green." In black tie and tails, GILBERT had performed "ambidextrous manipulations" with handkerchiefs, coins, and cards, then did "Mr. Gilbert's Original and Unique Card Rising Trick." After an intermission he unveiled the Flying Cage, the Oriental Casket, and the Diogenes Illusion. Madame Darsone then presented "Spiritualistic Phenomena of the Twentieth Century." And somewhere in the performance, if the Hyperion Theatre program is to be believed, there were handcuffs.

Progress may have lined the tracks, but this was still the heyday of Harry Houdini. Before Houdini, magic had been a marginal trade, slightly outré but never risky, never news. Magicians with single names made things appear or disappear, making it all look easy. Houdini made magic look hard. His were tricks of the do-not-try-this-at-home variety. Whether appearing in midwestern towns with water towers or in the capitals of Europe, Houdini made headlines. He escaped from bank vaults and maximum-security prisons. He emerged, dripping and shivering, from huge sealed canisters of milk. Hog-tied and shoved in a padlocked trunk, he was thrown into New York Harbor. He came up, waving both hands, in less than a minute. Thanks to Houdini, even ordinary magicians drew steady crowds, and an ordinary med student with a flair for showmanship could start a business selling magic tricks under the cryptic name of Mysto.

Depending on which magician you trusted, Gilbert either founded or joined the Mysto Manufacturing Company. He later said he started the company in 1908 with a partner, John Petrie. Yet Petrie claimed he'd been running Mysto since 1900. Gilbert, he said, simply signed on by offering a few of his tricks for mass production. Whichever story is true, while finishing med school, Gilbert began performing in New Haven shop windows selling Mysto's do-it-yourself illusions. His performances gathered crowds and sold out boxes of tricks, yet when Gilbert was too busy to perform, the same tricks sat on shelves. And sat. Gilbert and Petrie tried to hire other magicians to promote Mysto, but magicians were unreliable, showing up hungover if they showed up at all. So, to keep sales from slipping, Gilbert often took the train to New York to perform in Mysto's store on Broadway near Times Square. He was on his way there one morning in the fall of 1911 when he saw the future of the toy business out the window of a train.

As Manhattan's jagged skyline came into view across the East River, the train slowed to a crawl. Along the tracks, Gilbert noticed men putting up towers, twenty-foot-tall lattices of steel topped by triangular braces holding high-voltage lines. He had not been one of those boy engineers, always tinkering with tools. He had never been interested in building more than his own body, yet he was fascinated by the efficiency, the handiwork, the sheer heft of the girders. Wouldn't it be great fun to build towers like these in miniature? Wouldn't boys like him just itch to get their hands on them and start building bridges, cranes, and derricks right in their own living rooms? Before Gilbert could dream any further, the train crossed into Manhattan. He stored the idea in the back of his mind as he headed through streets that teemed with trolley cars, pushcarts, and an occasional automobile. But coming home that afternoon, with his sample case empty, he noted the new towers built that day and decided to play with his idea. Getting off the train in New Haven, he took the bus home and burst in the door. He told his wife, Mary, that they could have some real fun that night. Genuine fun. Did they have any heavy cardboard? Some strong scissors? A knife to make notches?

After dinner, the Gilberts cleared their kitchen table. Spreading out his crude materials, Gilbert and his wife cut girders out of shirt cardboards. They spent the evening making different lengths and shapes, curves and braces, all notched and perforated. After a few such evenings, he had a complete assortment of cardboard parts. He took his set to a machinist, who turned the prototype into steel. Now Gilbert knew he had something, something dandy, something crackerjack, something boys could use to build just like their dads did. But when he brought his set home and tried to square four girders together into a beam like the ones on the New York–New Haven line, something was wrong. The girders kept flaring out, flattening, falling apart. Finally, he got another idea. A thin lip along the edge of each strip made the girders overlap securely. Another visit to the machinist gave him what every boy builder needs, the perfect girder—long, flat, and flared at the edge. Fastening four of them with nuts and bolts, he made his first tower, just like the real ones on the railroad!

Over the next few weeks, Gilbert played like a kid while his wife watched. She had to leave the kitchen to nurse their daughter, but when she came back, she was delighted to see her husband so happy. Usually he worried, fretting about his business or the end of his athletic career. With his new toy, he was the boy she first met eight years earlier in an Oregon prep school. Mary Gilbert didn't even mind when Alfred stayed up till midnight bolting together dozens of tiny models. As he showed her each new toy, she praised it as if it were a life-size truck or wagon, not some toy. Mary would never be one to complain or question, yet she doubted her husband would do much with his new toy, aside from play with it. He wasn't in the toy business. He was in the magic business, and surviving in such a marginal trade seemed to a new mother to be enough magic for one family. She didn't want Alfred to find another trick up his sleeve, and neither did his partners.

Early in 1912, when Gilbert took the prototype of his Erector set down to the two-room Mysto shop, John Petrie and a third partner were skeptical. There were already a couple other construction toys on the market, they told Gilbert. And besides, mass-producing steel strips would require tool and die machines, sheet-metal presses, an entire factory. Gilbert shrugged off their concerns. They were "magic men," he realized. They wanted to stay small, focused on their narrow line. So like any boy with a dream, Gilbert turned to his father.

Frank Gilbert had come west when the West was the *West*. In 1869, when he was nineteen, he left his family's Indiana farm on a train to New York. There he took a steamer to Panama, crossed over the isthmus, then sailed to San Francisco. After hanging around the grungy, hilly city for a few weeks, Frank boarded a ship for Oregon. When he reached Portland, joining his older brother, who had come west on the Oregon Trail, the town had just 7,500 people. Frank worked odd jobs for a while before setting himself up in the insurance business. By the time his sons were born in the 1880s, he was a well-respected banker in Salem. Stalwart and sensible as a pin-striped vest, Frank Gilbert didn't raise any son of his to become a toy maker.

When Alfred entered Yale, Frank was proud but confused. He boasted to friends that his middle son was studying medicine; he only wished he could claim that Alfred would someday become a doctor. But the boy didn't seem to care about medicine at all. He was having a great time in college—joining societies, winning trophies, and striding beneath Yale's stately Gothic towers like some knight in olde England. Despite his magic and his athletics, he somehow passed his classes—barely—but he had no intention of practicing medicine. The M.D., he told his father, would help him become a college athletic director, yet Frank secretly hoped he could steer his son toward a more professional purpose. If not to become a doctor, why else would anyone study at one of the best and costliest medical schools in the country? Frank was sure that his sensible and highly driven boy would wise up once he graduated. Then came that afternoon in 1909, when his son first took him to the small Mysto factory a few miles from campus. It was one of the low points of Frank Gilbert's life. Here was an Olympic champion and Ivy League graduate proudly handing his father a nifty bunch of flowers that blossomed out of an empty vase. He had made the trick himself! He had dozens more like it! And he was in business selling them! Gee, son!

But Frank Gilbert had always backed his boys. Once, when watching Alfred wrestle, he got so excited he couldn't sleep for two nights, and his wife wouldn't let him attend any more matches. Whatever Frank Gilbert's sons did, they had to win at it. Hiding his disappointment at Alfred's strange new career, Frank wrote him a note for a $5,000 loan, at 5 percent interest. "Nothing my father ever did for me meant as much as that loan," Gilbert said.

A few years later, when Gilbert showed his dad the world's first Erector set, the old man saw its promise. Father and son became sole stockholders in the Mysto Manufacturing Company. Again, stories vary on just how that feat was performed. John Petrie blamed Frank Gilbert for convincing him to sign a release he didn't read, leaving him without any rights to trademarks, products, or the Mysto factory. Gilbert simply said his father bought out the partner for $4,500. The mystery of Mysto's takeover remains, but the company's struggles are recorded in its bottom line. Even in Houdini's day, there weren't enough magicians to make a magic firm highly profitable. The company's catalog listed scores of tricks—the Mysterious Rising Card, Mysto Multiplying Coin, the Diminishing Billiard Ball, the Magic Lighting Candles. Prices ranged from 25 cents to $95 a trick, but even at such rates, pulling a rabbit out of a hat was easy compared to turning a profit worthy of an Ivy Leaguer. In 1911 Mysto cleared $366.37. The following year, with Gilbert stumping the country to pitch his products, the company upped its profits to $7,437. Yet as he made his meager living, Gilbert invested much of his time and money in a single box from which would spring his fortune.

Mysto's tiny shop could never house the heavy machines needed to punch out steel girders, so Gilbert leased an old carriage factory on Foote Street, a few blocks north of his alma mater. For the next eighteen months, while Mary stayed home with their daughter, Gilbert put in long hours at the plant. There was an entire toy to make and market—trademarks to gather, patents to file, employees to hire. And Erector refused to stay one-dimensional. One day—Gilbert never said when or where—he got another "surefire" idea. He knew boys like himself would never be content to build models and let them sit on shelves. They would want to play with their constructions, using them to drive, hoist, power, and pull. This idea led to the painstaking development of a small motor, one powerful enough to impress a boy yet compact enough to run on batteries. The motor would enliven the dozens of models he was designing night after night—modest ones for the small fry, massive ones for their older brothers. Gilbert pushed himself to explore all the possibilities. Could he make a sled out of his girders? A band saw? London Bridge or a biplane just like the one the Wright Brothers had flown at Kitty Hawk just nine years earlier? "I put together hundreds of things," Gilbert remembered, "some of which worked and some of which didn't. I've often said that I have put together more bolts and nuts than any man alive or dead. And I had fun doing it, too." Armed with fun and a factory, feeling more content than he ever would again, Gilbert tinkered throughout 1912 and into the following year.

In the spring of 1913, when Gilbert took the train to the New York Toy Fair, it seemed as if American enterprise had reshaped his world in just eighteen months. Victorian fashion still held sway. Women wore bulky skirts and bustles topped by enormous feathered hats; men rarely went outside without a derby or bowler.

Yet everything had begun to move faster, get bigger, grow taller. "This is a get-things-done-quick age," one magazine noted. "It is a ready-to-put-on-and-wear-home age, a just-add-hot-water-and-serve age, a new-speed-record-every-day age, a take-it-or-leave-it-I'm-very-busy age." In Dearborn, Michigan, Henry Ford's new assembly line had cut the time it took to build a car from twelve hours to one and a half. As his train neared Manhattan, Gilbert surveyed a skyline etched by industry. From the Battery to the Upper West Side, cranes lifted girders to the top of buildings that soared twenty, thirty, sometimes fifty stories. The race was on to scrape the sky, and the winner was the Woolworth Building. Open for business that spring, the Woolworth Building was the world's tallest, standing 792 feet at its crown. Its owner, F. W. Woolworth, had paid for it in cash—$13.5 million earned from five-and-ten-cents stores. To be a builder, the skyscraper suggested, a boy didn't have to dig a canal. All he had to be was clever, inventive, and "wide-awake."

"Wide-awake" was the highest compliment a boy could earn in those days. Other boys were surely not sleepwalking, yet wide-awake boys were the ones crackling with enthusiasm, interested in everything, eager to get their hands on cars, planes, boats, and anything else that moved but didn't talk back. Wide-awake boys were the ones who got ahead, at least according to the best-selling boys' books of the time. Wide-awake Frank Merriwell attended prep school before going on to Yale. The Rover Boys—Tom, Dick, and Sam Rover—made every day an adventure in *The Rover Boys on the Ocean, The Rover Boys in the Jungle,* and eighteen other serials. And wide-awake boys like Tom Swift built their own inventions, making it look like child's play.

> "Ever invent an airship?" asked the rescued Mr. Sharp of Tom as the *Arrow* carried him towards Shopton.
> "No," replied the lad, somewhat surprised. "I never did."
> "I have," went on the balloonist. "That is, I've invented part of it. I'm stuck over some details. Maybe you and I'll finish it some day. How about it?"

"Maybe," assented Tom, who was occupied just then in making
a good landing. "I am interested in airships, but I never
thought I could build one."
"Easiest thing in the world," went on Mr. Sharp.

Whether making an airship, an Electric Runabout, or a Wizard
Camera, Tom Swift always did it himself, without any kits or
plans. When it came to real-life invention, however, many boys
would need help. As Gilbert left the train and gawked at the soaring, starry ceiling of the new Grand Central Station, he carried
the toy millions of boys would use to become Tom Swifts. Heft-
ing his heavy suitcase, he stepped onto Forty-second Street. Had
he turned north and made his way into Harlem, or strolled south
to the tenements of the Lower East Side, he would have seen the
flip side of progress, meeting boys who would never be able to afford his toys. But from Grand Central, Gilbert took the quickest
route, westward toward his hotel on Broadway. The industrial
age was sculpting the face of America. In his suitcase, Gilbert had
its building blocks.

Along with other toy makers, Gilbert took a room at the
Broadway Central. The room would double as a salesroom. The
American toy industry was still in its infancy. Nearly half of all
toys sold throughout the country were made in Germany, where
craft guilds churned out millions of hand-carved circus animals,
Noah's arks, drums and guns and dolls. With domestic toy sales
hovering around $10 million a year, promoters of the annual
New York Toy Fair couldn't afford to rent a hall, so manufacturers displayed samples in their rooms at the Broadway Central.
Spreading their toys across beds and carpets, they hosted buyers
who browsed like children at play. In 1913, Gilbert knew he'd
need a bigger room than he had used the previous year. For this
year's fair, along with Mysto's tricks, he had a thick wooden box
that weighed more than any other toy in any other bedroom. In
its top tray were dozens of inch-wide steel girders with triangu-

lar slots, just like those one might see along an electrified railroad track. There were red-spoked wheels that seemed ready to roll on a miniature Model T. There were pint-size brass pulleys, pinions, and plates punctured by neat rows of holes. Beneath the tray were axles, gears, and Gilbert's prize—his real battery-operated motor, "the motor with a punch."

Leaping around his room, Gilbert showed the toy men how to build the models he'd designed at his kitchen table. He set the windmill spinning. He made a bridge lift up. He hoisted an elevator up its shaft. Compared to the fair's other new toys—German-made Kewpie dolls and Steiff teddy bears—the Erector set seemed like boyhood in a box. Buyers bought, as did others at a toy fair in Chicago where Gilbert went next. Returning to New Haven, he had more orders than he could fill, but a loan from the aptly named Mechanic's Bank helped him boost production in time for Christmas sales. That fall, toy stores, hardware stores, and department stores began selling the first toy that did not talk down to kids or treat them like an audience at a Punch and Judy show, the first toy that let them build and design, think and imagine, fail and succeed.

Any boy opening one of these first Erector sets must have felt he'd just been handed the keys to the kingdom. Other toys of the time were one-trick ponies. Push a button, turn a crank, and your plaything played for you. But Erector was a different toy each time you opened the box. And that box! Most toys hid themselves. You had to yank them out, tear off a label, then search all over for a button or wind-up key to figure out what the hell they did. But Erector introduced itself to you. Flip up the lid, and the whole set spread out before your widening eyes. Pick up the pieces. Feel the heft of each girder, the teeth of each cogwheel, the sturdiness of the set's own screwdriver. See how the parts fit together, hand in glove, sprocket in gear. This was not a toy. This was how the world was put together. This was the stuff of rainy afternoons, after-school building binges, weeklong projects of power and pride. It almost seemed a shame that Mom and Dad liked Erector, too. It would have been much more fun if it had been forbidden.

And models! Unlike other toys—from aristocratic dollhouses to penny-apiece tops—Erector cut across class lines. Wanting all boys to become builders, Gilbert numbered his sets from 0 to 8. The smallest was basic and cheap. For 50 cents, a boy got a handful of parts in a cardboard box. After bolting together a chair, a ladder, a bed, and ten other models, the boy could save a buck and upgrade to the next set. And at each step up the Erector ladder, there were more models, models, models.

The No. 1 set built twenty-seven models. Cost—$1. No. 2, assembling thirty-nine models, was a bargain at $2. No. 3, for an additional buck, built fifty-five models. Then came the quantum leap to the sets for $5 and up, each with the first toy motor marketed in America. Gee, Dad! But before it could lift a drawbridge, the motor had to be assembled. Awww, Dad! A boy or his nearest mechanically minded relative had to wind copper wire around the armature, put together the base, fasten the field magnet in position, adjust the brushes. . . . Those who weren't up to the task could mail the parts to the big Mysto factory with the smokestack shown on the manual's inside cover. Enclose two quarters, and the motor would be assembled and shipped back the same day. Perhaps by Mr. Gilbert himself. Topping the Erector line was the bulky No. 8, with 6 gears, 4 propeller blades, 14 axles, 24 pulleys, 5 tires, 3 pinion gears, 32 perforated strips, 230 small screws, 200 twelve-inch girders, 222 shorter girders, a screwdriver, and a motor. Put them all together, and a boy could build one hundred different models, not to mention whatever implements of destruction he could design himself. Priced at $25, packaged in its own three-layered walnut case with lock and key, Erector was the classiest toy in a market dominated by what Gilbert derided as "flimsy flamsy gimcracks."

On Christmas morning in 1913, running late but catching up, boys across the country began building their own private twentieth centuries. Whether they lived in skyscrapered cities or on farms where the tallest structure was a windmill, Christmas brought them a model for the machine age. Hardly a boy who opened one of those first Erector sets survives today, but while unpacking it, many must have resembled the picture on the box. It shows a family gathered around a fireplace. Dad, seated in an armchair, is wearing a suit. Mom has on her modest housedress. Some stern uncle or older brother stands nearby. And on the floor are two boys in knickers building the future right in their own living room. To the boys who opened them, Erector sets made the rest of Christmas seem juvenile, silly, somehow beneath them. Yet they did more than that. Within three years, Erector had turned boxes of steel strips into more than $1 million in sales. And it had begun to change how toys and boys were made.

2

The Boy Problem

"Boys will be boys," as the saying goes, but during the decade before the dawn of the Erector set, boys were more than boys. They were a problem.

The problem was as old as boyhood itself. From Cain's slaying of Abel to the adventures of Huckleberry Finn, boys heard the call of their parents but heeded the call of the wild. The trouble with boys was noted in literature and lore, in philosophy and in nursery rhymes. "Of all the animals the boy is the most unmanageable," Plato wrote. And as every child knew, "Snips and snails and puppy dogs' tails, that's what little boys are made of." Before the industrial age, most boys' problems ended in a mother's shrug or a wife's sigh, yet in urban America of the 1900s, boys went well beyond snips and snails. On the streets of every city, gangs were powered by the untamed anger of boys. Boys whose fathers beat them when they could catch them. Boys who drifted from school because the teacher was "down on them." Boys whose mothers were widowed in a mill or mining accident, leaving them alone with five, seven, even nine children. Boys whose mothers asked them, "Why can't you be more like your sister?" but who couldn't because they were boys. Boys were

both an old problem and a new one. Fortunately, men were starting to take notice.

William Byron Forbush was a poet, a Congregational minister, and an inner-city missionary. His mission was to make the
world safe for boys and vice versa. Raised a devout Christian,
Forbush extended his mercy to boys, offering them understanding, kindness, even chivalry. In 1893 Forbush had started a boys'
group called the Knights of King Arthur. The Knights soon
spread into dozens of chapters around the country. Each turned
medieval fantasy into a round table of respect that gave boys the
boost they needed to grow up. With Forbush or another local
minister playing the role of Merlin, club members addressed each
other as page, squire, and knight. To move from lowly page to
knight, a boy had to earn 1,000 points, tallying one-eighth point
for each page read about a genuine hero. Rewards were earned
along the way. Finish a book about Lincoln, for example, and you
got to strut around calling yourself Sir Abraham Lincoln. More
than 125,000 boys became Knights of King Arthur before the
program lost favor to an upstart group called the Boy Scouts of
America. By then Forbush had become the nation's leading boy
booster. Boys were getting a bad rap, he preached. He had known
a few unrepentant thugs, but most boys deserved a more complex
description, one long enough to fill an entire book.

In 1901, Forbush published *The Boy Problem.* The book put
the specimen called "boy" under the social worker's microscope,
citing "ways in which boys spontaneously organize," and ways
adults might help them. Not content to examine "the boy problem" on city streets, the book concluded with chapters on "The
Boy Problem in the Church" and "The Boy Problem in the
Home." Forbush's book went through ten printings. The YMCA
made *The Boy Problem* required reading for its counselors. Psychologists and reformers took to the book's title and sent it up
like a signal flare. The warning was heeded. For the next dozen
years, concern about America's "boy problem" festered among
parents, teachers, and church groups. Literary journals ran arti-

cles entitled "The Sunday-School Boy Problem" and "What Is Wrong with Our Boys?" *Ladies' Home Journal* offered hints on "Why Boys Go Wrong." Other "boy books" followed Forbush's, including *Boy Training* and *Winning the Boy*. Some of this worry may have been alarmist, yet to anyone who knew a few or saw them prowling the streets, there was good reason to believe that boys were, if not a problem, at least a pain.

At the turn of the century, being a boy was hard work. The only tougher job was being a man, yet manhood came at an early age. Men worked twelve-to-fourteen-hour days. So did boys, some as young as ten or even eight years old. From old photos taken in sweatshops, coal mines, and mills, their grimy, leaden faces still accuse us. So do their words. "I worked every night till ten, eleven, and twelve o'clock," Jack London recalled of his job in a cannery. "My wages were small, but I worked such long hours that I sometimes made as high as $50 a month. Duty—I turned every cent over. Duty—I have worked in that hell hole for 36 straight hours, at a machine, and I was only a child." In cities, boys did the work no self-respecting man would take. Their jobs betrayed their status. At the head of the working class were bellboys, uniformed squadrons of spit-and-polish lads waiting on the wealthy in palatial hotels. A rung beneath were the newsboys in their grubby caps and baggy pants. On every urban street corner they shouted headlines—"Extra! Extra! Read All About It! McKinley Shot! Stranger Fires Two Bullets into His Stomach!" Lower on the ladder were messenger boys who ran through the streets, dodging trolleys while carrying mail and memos. At the bottom were bootblacks who spent their days bent double, buffing the footwear of gentlemen. And beneath the ladder lived street urchins who begged, stole, and cadged their subsistence from the kindness of strangers.

Being a boy was not only hard work; it was risky business. With no regard for their age, boys were crippled by machinery, buried in mines, or abandoned to slash and tear at each other in alleys. On the farm, a boy's life was less dangerous but no less labored. Men spent twelve hours a day behind a plow. So did boys, once they were big enough to hold the plow handles. Gilbert often spoke of summers he spent on his uncle George's farm in Hubbard, Oregon. Though still in his early teens, he worked alongside the older hired hands from daybreak to sunset, plowing behind a pair of horses, threshing, milking, loading hay. Later, he would turn the toil into a moral lesson. "At last the harvest was over," he wrote in *Erector Tips,* his magazine for owners of Erector sets. "My hands were calloused and my muscles were like iron. That's the way to get strong, boys." But Gilbert didn't tell boys how he'd been exploited. He expected to earn $75 for the summer like the rest of the workers, but after three months of drudgery, his uncle gave him just $15 and a dog. Gilbert never returned to his uncle's farm. The next summer, he got a job as a flagman on a Northern Pacific Railroad crew surveying the woods of northern Idaho, making a dollar a day and wrestling all comers as the crew moved from town to town.

For Gilbert and other boys in rural America, the only relief from hard work came from hard play. In small towns, their mischief was the usual small-town stuff—outhouses tipped over, tomatoes well aimed at an enemy, pigtails dipped in ink. Urban boys, however, had a way of becoming everyone else's problem. Boys outnumbered men in many cities, especially in tenements and jails. These days, five times as many boys as girls commit crimes, but in 1900 the ratio was fifty to one. Just what *was* wrong with our boys? Boosters like William Byron Forbush were quick to note that the boy problem was really a parent problem. Parents, especially fathers, weren't spending enough time with their boys. Temptation waited for the boy left alone. Saloon keepers served him liquor on demand. Drug dealers saw him as a steady customer. Gamblers found him an easy mark. There seemed no end to the problems a boy could be. Whatever ailed America's boys, they weren't likely to wise up without the help of men who remembered what it was like to be one of them.

Yet so few men seemed to remember. That was part of the problem.

Every man has survived boyhood, but not every man has learned from the harrowing experience. Perhaps A. C. Gilbert became an apostle of boyhood because he never forgot his own. Or maybe he forgot just enough, looking back through the filter of memory to an idyllic youth of games, pranks, and an unbridled winning streak. For whatever reason, once he began selling Erector sets, Gilbert started to champion an upbringing quite unlike that of boys on the street. "I had the happiest boyhood of anybody I ever knew," he remembered. "Nobody ever had so much fun, good clean fun, I mean."

While other boys were raising hell, Gilbert enjoyed a boyhood that, by today's standards, appears innocent, contrived, and just plain corny. He was born February 15, 1884, in Salem, Oregon, but when he was eight, his family moved to Idaho. In both states, he seems equally to have grown up in a Boy Scout manual. "Gosh" and "golly" may never have been in his vocabulary, but the words haunt the stories he told boys in *Erector Tips*. Should boys have taken him at his word? Did he really have his own Indian pony? (Gosh!) Did he try to parachute off his family's barn? (Golly!) There is no particular reason to be sure. Aside from a few old photos of him flexing his biceps or posing with handmade medals, Gilbert's reminiscences are the only record from his boyhood in the Pacific Northwest at the close of the nineteenth century. The timing of his reminiscences does not always fit neatly into a chronology. Some of his stories contradict others. Yet because the stories are more naive than self-aggrandizing, there is no particular reason to doubt them. Taken together, however, do they constitute the entire picture or just the frame?

For most adults, frontier life was harsh and brutal. Its days of isolated toil were softened only by Saturday-evening dances or Sunday box socials. Some parents took the strain out on their children, refusing to spare the rod. Yet for a favored few, freedom was the fringe benefit of living so far from the maddening crowds and so achingly dependent on one's own mettle. Gilbert seems to have been one of those favored few. Born to nurturing parents, surrounded by a loving, extended family, he grew up lean, strong, and as well suited to the outdoors as a redwood. Reason insists that he must have known the same hardships as other boys— brutal bullies, cruel teachers, nagging doubts and fears. Yet the boyhood he described, the one he wanted all "Gilbert boys" to mirror, did not include such trials. By not mentioning hardship, he did not make it disappear from his past. He merely put adversity in its place, making achievement that much sweeter. And in putting his boyhood on a pedestal, it didn't hurt to have a few genuine Tom Sawyer stories to share, to have them set in the old West, and to have a folksy nickname. As an adult, Gilbert was known to friends and employees as A. C. His wife and parents alone called him Alfred, a name he seems to have despised. But from boyhood through college, he was simply "Gillie."

All the adults in Moscow, Idaho, were relieved when Gillie built an athletic club in his barn. Moscow, a town of 2,000 people, lay at the base of Idaho's Panhandle, just a quick gallop from the Washington border. This was Palouse Country, its wheat fields and fluffy sky offering a welcome rest for pioneers coming west out of the Bitterroot Mountains. Work was relentless on the frontier in the 1890s, when Idaho was the nation's newest state. The University of Idaho, though it had just forty students, gave Moscow a touch of class, but most men worked grueling jobs in lumber camps up in the Palouse Hills. Others farmed or toiled in the Moscow Iron Works. The rest found employment downtown in brick storefronts whose turrets, arched windows, and bronze cupolas made Moscow resemble a model-train layout. There was a general store, a jeweler, a grocer, a blacksmith, a livery stable, and the First National Bank, where Frank Gilbert worked as cashier. And although the town's good Christians didn't mention them,

Moscow also had gambling halls, saloons, and one or two whorehouses, licensed and legal. Up and down muddy Main Street, horses, including the spotted Appaloosas bred by Nez Percé Indians, stood hitched to railings along wooden sidewalks. By frontier standards, nothing was unusual about Moscow. Moose and elk occasionally ambled through town. A man riding horseback sometimes got bucked off and broke his neck. A young woman suddenly left town, pursued by rumors. Moscow was a typical frontier town, from its men and women right down to its boys.

They ran in packs, bunches of scruffy runts in hand-me-down clothes. At the head of one pack was Gillie. Though shorter than most, he was plainly the leader. He could talk the other boys into anything, even chores. Each winter when he had to haul firewood up a hill to his house, he rigged up a wooden "chute-the-chute," offering a wild ride downhill to any boy who helped him bring the wood up. A master salesman, Gillie could organize his friends into any club, whip them into a frenzy with any contest, lead the charge in any rescue.

Take the Red Flag Fire Department. Ten-year-old Gillie and his friends spent weeks making a fire station in the Gilbert barn. They furnished sleeping rooms upstairs in the haymow. With Frank Gilbert's grudging permission, they cut a hole in the floor and erected a pole to slide down. Finally, they commandeered a wagon and equipped it with 100 feet of garden hose. The department was ready, yet its first run was almost its last. Racing out of the barn to the clanging of a bell, all the firemen made it down the pole, except one. Sugar Puss, so named because he often wolfed down whole handfuls of honey and other sweets, was too fat to slip through the hole. He got stuck, started crying, and had to be rescued by adults, the little baby. But the fiasco didn't deter Gillie.

Next came the great Indian rescue. Needing a damsel in distress, Gillie talked one fireman into betraying every frontier tenet of boyhood. Someone had to put on his sister's clothes. Who would it be? It took some salesmanship, but Gillie got one boy to don a dress. Then several others dressed like Sioux in full feathers and war paint. Whooping it up, they kidnapped the damsel, then for good measure set fire to some leaves. "She" played her part, screaming for help, but when the Red Flag Fire Department came running, 100 feet of hose was not enough. One fireman yanked too hard. The hose ripped the faucet off the wall. Water spurted everywhere except in the vicinity of the brushfire. Once again, adults had to intervene. As Gilbert later wrote, "This unfortunate episode put an end to the Red Flag Fire Department much to the disgust of its members."

When not playing with other boys, Gilbert spent his spare time making magic. Selling subscriptions to a boys' magazine, he earned his first magic kit. Soon he was making cards disappear and coins vanish. By the time he was eleven, he was the best boy magician in town. Then he met Hermann the Great. The traveling magician, with a pointed black beard and black cape, came through Moscow on the vaudeville circuit, and Gilbert got a ticket. After Hermann had performed several tricks, he began calling for volunteers. Finally, he picked "that fine looking boy on the aisle." Onstage, Gilbert smiled as Hermann pulled a rabbit, a bunch of bananas, and silver dollars from Gilbert's pockets. Finally, he turned to the boy and asked, "Well, son, don't you wish you could do things like that?" Gilbert coolly answered, "I can." He then began backpalming cards and making other items disappear, stealing the show and winning a backstage invitation to meet Hermann. Gilbert the Great took the pro's advice, practicing his magic hours each day, but he also practiced being a boy until he mastered that, too.

After neighbors complained about boys racing trikes at 4:00 A.M., it was politely suggested that Gillie's megawatt energy be channeled into athletics. He and his gang soon joined the nation on its health kick. In the 1890s, Americans sought exercise for the fun of it. Bicycles sold by the millions. A new game called basketball spread across college campuses, while baseball and football dominated the fields of summer and fall. Muscles were in fashion. Some boxers still fought bare-knuckled. Bodybuilders with handlebar mustaches posed in tank tops. On kitchen tables, John Harvey Kellogg's new breakfast cereals helped people slim down, while C. W. Post's Postum gave them a healthy substitute for coffee. To counter the effects of work in factories and mills, doctors prescribed physical culture, a regimen based on bag punching and calisthenics with heavy Indian clubs. Physical culture's motto was "Care for the body, settle the mind," but a more telling slogan for the era came from Gillie's idol, Theodore Roosevelt.

Roosevelt had been a sickly child. At three, he began suffering violent asthma attacks, mostly at night. His father walked the floor, holding his wheezing son upright so he could breathe. "Teedie" also had chronic stomach pain, headaches, colds, fevers. He walked on spindly legs, hoisted himself on stick arms. When Teedie was twelve, his father, an aristocratic, bearded bear of a man, took him aside. "Theodore," he said, "you have the mind but you have not the body, and without the help of the body the mind cannot go as far as it should. You must *make* your body." Theodore began lifting weights in his own makeshift athletic club, setting up backyard track meets, setting himself rigorous physical tests. After college, told he had to take it easy or his frail heart would kill him, Roosevelt drove himself harder—climbing the Matterhorn, roaming the Plains on horseback, sometimes riding seventy miles in a day. From such self-made manhood came Roosevelt's signature phrase, "the strenuous life." This life of labor and effort led to "that highest form of success which comes not to the man who desires mere easy peace but the man who does not shrink from danger, from hardship, or from bitter toil, and who out of these wins the splendid ultimate triumph."

Gillie's own strenuous life began in the barn that had been a fire station. At twelve, he formed the Moscow Athletic Club in his father's barn. He lined the building with posters from the Barnum & Bailey Circus, then installed a punching bag, climbing ropes, a chinning bar, and a set of Indian clubs. The Moscow Athletic Club had a dozen members, but only one worked out for hours each day. Only one became so skilled at the punching bag— hammering it with fists, elbows, shoulders, even blindfolded— that he ran away from home to join a traveling minstrel show, billing himself "The Champion Boy Bag Puncher of the World." Frank Gilbert had to track down his son in Lewiston, a day's ride south of Moscow, and bring him home. There were no lectures, no belts laid across a bare backside. As the father of three sons— the elder, quiet Harold, this middle sparkplug, and a third much younger and softer—Frank Gilbert understood boys better than that. But neighbors shook their heads.

When he was fourteen, Gillie began organizing track meets and soliciting sponsors. "Now, Mr. Grocer," he said, standing in the store with a pack of friends. "If you will give us some money or some goods for prizes for our Athletic Contest, we will give you a good advertisement." Then he introduced Mr. Grocer to a loudmouth named Sam. Sam put his hands to his mouth and bel- lowed, "The Jackson grocer gave us a dollar to print the pro- grams!" Promising to have Sam shout the same before the crowd at the meet, Gillie got his dollar. Moving down Main Street, he sought other sponsors. The town printer donated his services. A jeweler gave him the backs of old watches. Drilled with a hole and laced with string, these became the gold medals for a meet held on Moscow's baseball diamond. And who won six of seven events, including sprints, hurdles, the shot put, and the hammer throw? The shortest, slightest boy in the group. He won them so easily he took up a more challenging event he'd seen during a uni- versity track meet.

The man who invented the Erector set made his first inven- tion as a boy. When Gillie took up the sport, every vaulter in the world used a spiked pole, sticking the spike into the ground just before taking off. Gillie had no spiked pole, just an old cedar post he "borrowed" from a farmer's split-rail fence, then sanded to his satisfaction. Needing something to keep his pole from slipping on the grass, he dug a hole in the ground and began jamming his

fence post into it with every vault. After several falls and splinters
he cleared five feet. Soon he was approaching six feet, seven, even
eight. The vaulting technique he invented and popularized a
decade later is still used today by vaulters clearing twenty feet.

By 1901, when his idol reached the White House, Gillie had
become one of America's most promising athletes. Attending a
prep school affiliated with Pacific University, near Portland,
he captained the football and track teams, won the Northwest
wrestling championship, and headlined gymnastics meets. Only
eighteen, he was used to seeing his name on posters plastered
across Portland.

With baseball and boxing the only professional sports, almost any contest could draw a crowd, so Gillie tumbled, leaped,

COME! COME!
ENTERTAINMENT
GIVEN BY THE
Riverside Bicycle Club
AT RIVERSIDE HALL
Saturday Evening, March 22

GILBERT AND SEWELL
*Champion Tumblers and all round Athletes of
Pacific University. Come and see them!*

Music? You bet! Singing? Well, I guess! Recitations? You know it!
Grub! Grub! Grub!
*After the program, an OYSTER SUPPER will be served.
Come! You need the fun; and help a good cause.*

DON'T FORGET: MARCH 22, 1902

and hurled himself into local fame. Cigar-chomping men in bowlers hurrahed as he showed off his prowess. In a typical show, he did flips and somersaults, twirled Indian clubs, punched the bag, spun on the horizontal bar, flew on a trapeze, then for good measure wrestled a classmate. Whenever possible, he tackled some obscure world record. In one frantic stint, he did more chin-ups—forty—than anyone in history. He set other records for the rope climb (twenty-five feet in seven seconds) and the long dive. The latter event required him to race down a runway, leap as if long-jumping, and land headfirst in a sand pit. On June 14, 1902, Gilbert took the world's longest dive, clearing fifteen feet and nine inches before gravity sent him skidding along the ground—all in all, a tough way to get your name in the papers.

During two summers with the gymnastics team at the Chautauqua Institute in New York, Gillie met coaches from Yale. They encouraged him to enroll there, and with support from his father and money he'd earned on his uncle's farm, he entered Yale Medical School in 1905. At Yale, then a dominant force in amateur athletics, he lettered in wrestling, gymnastics, and track. He won the national intercollegiate wrestling championship, middleweight division. And he vaulted.

On May 31, 1906, Gilbert stood on a track before 40,000 fans at New York's Celtic Park. Going into a crouch, pole in his hands, he prepared to soar higher than any human had ever gone on his own power. Rising, he started out slowly but was soon sprinting down the runway. He planted his bamboo pole and let its stiffness pull him off the ground. His legs swung upward. Soaring, turning, he arched over the bar, then released the pole, letting his hands fly free. He thudded into the sawdust below, having cleared twelve feet three inches—another national championship, another world record. That same year, "athletic men" judged Gilbert's physique—"a mass of springs"—to be the best in the world. In one photo, he posed shirtless, his arms modestly behind him, his face handsome but as blank as ever, his chest and biceps worthy of Michelangelo's *David*. Later this physique would propel him to a record twelve feet seven inches and on to the Olympics. The boy had become a man. Gillie was now "Gil," and, once he began running his own company, A. C.

>>—

Having driven himself from boy to man, Gilbert felt well suited to do the driving for other boys. While at Yale and while starting Mysto, he did not concern himself much with the younger set. He was no missionary like Forbush, no booster like the YMCA counselors who wrestled with the boy problem. But then he invented a toy that every boy wanted. At an age when many men begin sharing their secrets with sons, Gilbert had only a daughter. He did have Erector, however. Hence, he had an audience. He began speaking paternally to that audience in his first ad in November 1913, which proclaimed, "Hello Boys! Make Lots of Toys."

Before Gilbert began advertising, toy ads were like toys themselves—small, formulaic, and some adult's idea of what a kid wanted. Each Christmas season, these ads filled the corners of the nation's very few children's magazines, monthly journals of innocence and fluff. Yet although the ads were read by boys and girls, most were aimed at parents.

"FLEXIBLE FLYER: The ideal Christmas gift for boys and girls. Nowadays they want more than a steering sled. . . ."

"Have You Got a Young EDISON? If so, the most appropriate present to him will be our Static Wimshurst Machine. Gives a 3-inch spark. . . . Harmless and foolproof. The most appropriate present for the boy."

Gilbert's ads were different. Like some new kid on the block eager to win friends, he promised nonstop excitement. Slipping in under parents' radar, he made his promise directly to those who did the begging behind the buying. The first Erector ad was just two inches tall, hidden deep inside *Youth's Companion*, the magazine whose subscription premium had started Gilbert's magic career. Yet the pitch seemed to have been written by a kid for a kid. "It's fun to read my new 24-page booklet full of pictures of toys easy to make quickly with the Mysto Erector, the Toy that resembles structural steel. Has 20% more parts than any similar toy. You alone can build big towers, bridges, cars to go by little electric motor, etc. My real square steel girders look like the big bridges and steel buildings. It's great fun. Toy dealers sell it: $1.00 and up. Write me now for my book." The ad was signed "A. C. Gilbert, President, The Mysto Mfg. Co, 56 Foote St., New Haven, Conn."

"More parts than any similar toy"? Gilbert claimed to have invented Erector out of whole cloth, or steel as the case may be, but as his Mysto partners had warned, other construction toys had beaten him to the market. The first was Meccano, sold in England since 1901 and in America as of 1910. But wimpy little Meccano was made of tinplate or nickel-plated brass, not "structural steel." Besides, Meccano was British. Could a boy in Ohio or Kansas hope to solve his "problem" by building some bloody "lorry" or petrol-driven car with a "boot" and a "bonnet"? Stiffer competition for Erector came from two American-made construction toys. Struktiron had real steel girders, gears, and axles. The American Model Builder offered curved girders enabling boys to build clocks, printing presses, and "hundreds of other models that you can really operate." So how did the Erector set destroy the competition, becoming the most successful, most talked-about toy of its time? Because Gilbert made himself part of the package.

"I was convinced that boys became interested and excited when a *person,* not a corporation, spoke to them," Gilbert remembered. His ads, soon filling full pages, began boasting of his insider knowledge, greeting boys as his "boy friends," even "chums." "Hello Boys! Now for Fun. I guess all you boys know me well enough to know that when I say 'fun,' I mean the kind of fun that you and I know is real fun. Not the namby-pamby fun that some grown folks think is fun for a boy, but play that's real, play that's got a punch to it—play in which you *build* things, *make* things, and *do* things, just like genuine man stuff."

Throughout his career, Gilbert trusted what he called "practical boy psychology." If he liked to play with something, he figured boys would like it, too. Never mind that he was a husband, father, and Yale M.D. Now twenty-nine going on nine, Gilbert was the oldest boy in America, one who still knew what made other boys stop shouting and listen up. Meccano or Struktiron boasted that their models were "mechanically correct," but only Erector talked the talk—the boy talk of power, envy, and success. "Erector models are the biggest, firmest, strongest and most finished," ads boasted. "There is much more equipment in Erector sets than in other boxes at the same price." "Think of the fun building battleships, torpedo boats, Brooklyn Bridges with third-rail cars run by a real motor—skyscrapers with running elevators—electric run sand shovels that dig just like the Panama Canal dredges."

Because Gilbert thrived on competition, he knew every "live-wire boy" would, too. "We are conducting a contest for the newest, most ingenious, and original models," his first manual announced. "Write for information regarding contests, prizes, etc." Winners of the first Erector contest received premiums ranging from $15 cash to a $1 Erector set, but boys hadn't seen anything yet. The following fall, *Erector Tips* announced that "over a thousand boys from all parts of Christendom sent in drawings, photographs, sketches, blueprints, and descriptions of hundreds of models." The race to be a real Gilbert boy was on. The winners so far were two lads from New Haven whose first-place entry was an Erector battleship with dual smokestacks, three decks, and the Stars and Stripes waving off the bow. Other entries ranged from innovative designs to unabashed nostalgia. Gilbert's girders may have been bulky, but aspiring engineers twisted and bolted them into surprising configurations. Radial drill presses, hay wagons, butter churns, barber's chairs, monoplanes, moving-picture cameras, torpedo boats, doll carriages—"Fun?" one ad asked. "I should say so!"

When not a boy winning over other boys, Gilbert doubled as a parent speaking to other parents. In 1915 he tapped the zeitgeist that had been building since the dawn of *The Boy Problem.* That Christmas season, he ran a full-page ad in *Good Housekeeping,* a magazine read by absolutely no sons but by plenty of mothers whose boys had gone wrong. The ad showed two lads building a railroad trellis big enough to rival those at Grand Central. Atop the ad a banner headline proclaimed: "Solves the Boy Problem." In the ad, Gilbert assured mothers that everything would be all right. Their sons might be delinquent, distant, or just bouncing off the wall, but someone understood. "I know that it is a problem for mothers to find something which not only amuses and entertains a vigorous boy but also has educational value," the ad began. "Erector has solved this problem for thousands of parents. It appeals to every boy's idea of fun and teaches him the principles of construction and engineering."

Gilbert did not solve the boy problem alone. The success of Erector owed as much to the tenor of the times as to its inventor's cunning. Historians define those times with a single word— *progressive.* During the Progressive era, the nation seemed energized, as if activism were its birthright. Pick an issue, and there was a citizen's group to address it. Name a cause, and there was a crusade. By contemporary standards, the era wasn't all that progressive. Middle-class women still toiled in the home, while working-class women sewed in sweatshops. The South was scarred by frequent lynchings. The North, from its social clubs to its summer camps, was segregated by creed and class. The West was besieged by labor violence, claiming dozens of lives in logging and mining camps. Yet victims were finding a voice. The nation took steps to purify its food, bust its trusts, and clean up cities mired in corruption and graft. The era would shape America's social agenda for the next fifty years, its movements leading to Prohibition, woman suffrage, the first income tax, and the forty-hour workweek. All these causes were hotly contested, yet one on which the nation agreed was the need to save its children.

By 1915, the burden of being a boy had been lightened. Juvenile courts were established in all but a few states. The federal government had created a Children's Bureau. Every state had passed some kind of child labor law, halving the number of children working in factories and mines. Freed from work, adolescents gathered in the streets. Then, when truant officers loomed, kids decided they might as well stay in school. High school had become the country's fastest-growing institution. In 1880, only 110,000 students had attended high school; now enrollment neared 2 million. Suddenly, kids had a lot of time on their hands. One-trick toys couldn't fill an afternoon, but one toy, peddled by a man who seemed to know just what a boy wanted, offered the chance to make lots of toys. And lots of boys, or their concerned mothers, bought Gilbert's paternal pitch.

In the year before Erector debuted, the Mysto Manufacturing Company sold $59,000 worth of magic tricks. Gilbert's salary was $125 a month. With Erector in its line, sales more than doubled and profits multiplied six times. Directors, including Gilbert's father, voted their president a $1,500 bonus. Two years after Erector appeared, Mysto's profits were up 1,800 percent. The sudden success didn't result from a nationwide craze for Diminishing Billiard Balls or Magic Lighting Candles. It was the little box of steel girders that catapulted its inventor into the role of spokesman for toys and mentor for his chums who loved them. The boy problem had not been solved. Some argue that it is still with us. But woe to the lad, confronted by the march of technology, who did not have a trusty set that "appeals to every boy's idea of fun." There was no telling what he might do.

✦

By 1915, with World War I raging, adults had better things to fret about than boys. Books and magazine articles no longer mentioned the boy problem. Boys were still being boys, but their motives had changed. Early that winter, two teenage boys went on a rampage through Portland, Oregon. They stole a car, then ca-

reened through the streets holding up women at gunpoint. The
pair was quickly captured, tried, and sentenced. Yet unlike other
urban toughs, these boys did not steal because they were angry,
distant, or abused. One stole because he wanted to tinker.

"I really didn't think of the money," said Earl Riley, listed in
the newspaper as "Portland's boy auto bandit, highway robber
and desperado." "I have always been interested in mechanics. I
wanted to take an auto apart and examine its engine. Not having
a car or the money to buy one, I went out and stole it." As he
went off to jail, Riley blamed his parents. He vividly recalled the
day when his father had led him through the toy department of a
major store. There he saw a tin model of an automobile engine on
sale for 98 cents. He begged for it, but his father refused. "If I had
been given that engine," Riley said, "and my love for the mechanical had been fostered instead of crushed, I might be a good
mechanic today, instead of a convict!"

The urge to tinker went unchecked, so when his friend asked
him to steal a car, Riley agreed. "I didn't want to go, but the auto
he pointed out to me lured me into the agreement. I didn't care
about the money we might get. I wanted to manage that engine.
So I hopped in and did the driving while Jesse would get out and
hold up the girls. I had more fun starting and stopping that engine
than I did with all the money we got." Riley concluded his speech
with a caution. "I want to warn all the parents to find out the
thoughts and ambitions of their boys and help them along the
right lines. Don't let the boy run wild."

This cautionary tale made no headlines, just a small notice in
a few papers. One, however, was the *New Haven Times Leader*,
where Gilbert read it. The message was not lost on Erector's inventor. Gilbert reprinted the article in *Erector Tips*. Beneath a
bold headline, "Boy Bandit Reproaches Parents: They Wouldn't
Buy Him Instructive Playthings So He Stole," the article ran
without comment. The problem, by then, was obvious, the solution evident to anyone who was wide-awake.

> *What are you able to build with your blocks?*
> *Castles and palaces, temples and docks.*
> *Rain may keep raining, and others go roam,*
> *But I can be happy and building at home.*
> —ROBERT LOUIS STEVENSON

3

Prizes! Prizes! Prizes!

To use a proper Victorian expression, the 1908 Olympics were an untidy affair. Partisan, political, and tainted by foul play, they were most un-British. For the 120 athletes on the American team, including the world record holder in the pole vault, the only fun was the getting to London.

The S.S. *Philadelphia* steamed out of New York Harbor on June 27. That same morning two contractors and an architect were hoisted 700 feet above Manhattan. Atop the steel skeleton of the Metropolitan Life Building, they drove a golden rivet to complete the first phase of construction. Then, clinging to the girders, they broke a champagne bottle on the building. It was a clear, breezy day, and from the dock on Vesey Street, Gilbert could see the building—8,000 tons of steel girders foreshadowing his future. Yet as crowds along the quay waved flags and cheered the Olympians, he cast his gaze toward England and his goal. "Thirteen feet was my goal at the Olympics," he recalled. "I wanted to be the first man to vault that high, and there was good reason to expect that I might be." He had already topped thirteen feet in practice, and Frank Gilbert had promised him a $100 gold coin if he did it for the record in the Olympics. But before clear-

ing any bar, he would have to dodge the roadblocks British officials were about to put in the way of every American favorite.

On board the *Philadelphia*, passengers hoped this voyage
would not be as ill-fated as America's last trip to the Olympics.
Only two years earlier, the team bound for unofficial games in
Athens had steamed into troubled waters. One day out of New
York, a rogue wave swept over the deck. Several athletes were
smashed against the bulwarks and deck rails. Six were badly hurt.
One dislocated a shoulder while saving a distance runner from
being swept overboard. But the *Philadelphia* had smooth sailing
across the North Atlantic. On their second day out, passengers
were entertained by the cosmos. That afternoon, they sailed
through a partial solar eclipse, squinting at it through smoked
glass. On other afternoons, American athletes entertained passengers with workouts on deck. Some jogged in formation, while
others did acrobatics, to the delight of onlookers. Gilbert and
hurdler Forrest Smithson repeated a routine they had perfected
while headlining gymnastics meets in Oregon. Defying the ship's
gentle roll, Smithson lay on his back while Gilbert climbed on his
hands and did a handstand. Restless and bored, Gilbert also raced
one of the crew in a rope climb to the top of a mast, winning
handily. And one evening he performed his magic in the ship's
dining room. Pulling rabbits out of hats and various coins out of
thimbles, he drew gasps from people who wondered whether
they would someday hear more about this young man from Yale.
Later, Gilbert won the ship's shuffleboard tournament although
he had never played before.

After a quiet crossing, the *Philadelphia* docked in Southamp-
ton, and the fun was over. To host the games, the British had built
the largest arena in Europe. The 68,000-seat stadium in West
London suggested that these Olympics, held at the height of the
British Empire, would not be another American rout. Four years
earlier, few countries could afford to send full teams all the way
to St. Louis, leaving the Americans to win seven of every eight
medals. The London games would be worldwide Olympics, fea-

turing more than 2,000 athletes from twenty-two countries. They
would be fair and inspirational, even helping "to dissipate causes
of war," one magazine predicted. Yet war by other means was
about to break out on the field.

The rancor surfaced during the opening ceremony. Flags
flew. Bands marched. And when the Americans entered the stadium, their flag was nowhere to be found. Officials apologized
for the "oversight," and the U.S. team marched behind a flag
loaned by a spectator. The team soon took revenge. As nation after nation strode past King Edward VII and Queen Alexandra,
each dipped its colors. Yet American flag bearer Ralph Rose, a
shot-putter, was of Irish descent. Furious that Ireland's athletes
had been forced to compete on the British team, Rose refused to
lower the Stars and Stripes. "This flag dips for no earthly king,"
he told sportswriters, starting a tradition American Olympians
still follow. The next day, the British press denounced such
"sheer caddish, boorish manners." The games had begun.

From the opening gun, it was clear who was running this
show. British judges openly coached U.K. athletes. Dressed nat-
tily in bowlers and dark sport coats, the judges yelled encouragement through their megaphones as they rooted for passing
sprinters or ran alongside distance runners. Rules forbade certain
uniforms and footwear—except for British squads. Officials met
in secret to match sprinters and hurdlers for heats. Fast Americans eliminated each other while slower runners raced the Brits.
London newspapers touted the promise of British athletes, saving special rancor for the damned Yanks, whose attitude of "win,
tie, or wrangle" did not match Britain's gentlemanly sportsmanship. In the stands, journalists griped, Americans had the nerve to
sit together, cheering and making "disgusting noises and cries."
Those who stood for "The Star-Spangled Banner" were told, "Sit
down!" and one young boy waving the Stars and Stripes had it
yanked out of his hands. Appalled and homesick, Gilbert wished
he hadn't postponed his wedding to come to the Olympics. "You
don't know how much I love the American States after a visit

here," he wrote to his fiancée, Mary Thompson, waiting for him in Seattle. "There's only one America and you can't appreciate it thoroughly until you have visited such a country as England. English people haven't anything to be proud of, not even themselves. Contrary to the generally accepted opinion they are the poorest sportsmen in the world."

The sportsmanship continued on the track. In the 400-meter final, a lone Brit was to race against three Americans. Local papers warned that the Yanks would doubtless conspire against the home favorite, and the U.S. coach, wanting no hint of unfairness, told his athletes to stay clear of the Limey. But coming into the final turn, the American J. C. Carpenter swept wide in his lane and took a solid lead. Instantly, judges ran onto the track, brandishing megaphones. "No race!" one called out. "Foul work on the part of the Americans!" Before Carpenter could cross the finish line, a judge snapped the tape and voided the race. Fans hooted, urging their officials to disqualify the "dirty Americans." Carpenter insisted his opponent had plenty of room, but he was disqualified. When the race was run again, the other two Americans refused to compete, ceding the British runner the gold medal,

But the 400-meter was just the warm-up for the strangest marathon ever held. On race day, the weather was as un-British as the hospitality—hot and humid. As runners spread out along the course, the favorites soon dropped out. Coming into the final mile, the race was between Italy's Dorando Pietri, a twenty-two-year-old candy maker from Capri, and Johnny Hayes, a clerk at Bloomingdale's in New York. Pietri had a commanding lead, yet approaching the stadium, he began to stagger. Officials examined him and found him exhausted, nearly delirious. They gave him a shot of strychnine, then thought to be a stimulant in small doses. Entering the stadium, Pietri turned left instead of right, wobbling all over the track. He fell, got to his feet, fell again. Judges rubbed his legs, lifted him, and sent him in the proper direction, but he fell three more times. He was lying in a heap thirty yards from the tape when Hayes steamed into the stadium, unfazed by heat or distance. British officials weren't about to see an American win, so they hoisted the limp Pietri and escorted him across the finish line.

It took several hours for anyone in charge to admit mistakes had been made. The Italian flag flew over the victory stand, even as Pietri was rushed unconscious to the hospital, where he nearly died. Finally, grudgingly, judges disqualified their winner and the victory went to Hayes, who was roundly booed. The British thing to do, sportswriters said, would have been to give the plucky Italian his due and his gold medal, but a dirty American would never be such a "sufficiently good sportsman."

By the time the pole vault began, Gilbert had absorbed the mean spirit of the games. He had been told he could not vault using the indented box he had invented back in Oregon. Vaulters all over the world were now using such boxes, made of metal instead of dirt, but because the British and a favored Canadian still used spiked poles, officials declared that all competitors would use them. American vaulters considered going home early, but Gilbert decided that "direct action might get results." On the morning of his first heat, he stopped at a hardware store and bought a small hatchet. Coming onto the field, he hid it under his sweater. When no one was looking, he walked to the standard and crouched down. He was hacking a notch in the fine English turf when he was spotted. Judges surrounded him. The groundskeeper seized the hatchet, and a bobby began to lead Gilbert away. Stone-faced as always, Gilbert insisted that the rules be read aloud. They were. No rule required spiked poles, yet judges declared it was the "English custom" to vault with them, and custom would be respected.

Dejected but determined, Gilbert gave up his goal of clearing thirteen feet and earning $100 from his father. With a spike driven into his pole, he began vaulting. Feeling "awkward as a calf," he managed to win his first heat, clearing twelve feet even. Edward Cooke of Cornell won the second heat at twelve feet, two inches, giving the two Americans the field to themselves. Later that July afternoon, Gilbert again topped twelve feet, the only man to do so in the finals, but just when he thought he had won the gold, judges set the bar even higher. "What's the matter?" one asked as Gilbert headed back to the locker room. "Don't you want to try to win?"

"What are you talking about?" Gilbert answered. "I won. I cleared twelve feet. Cooke didn't."

Judges told him he would have to clear twelve feet, two inches, Cooke's top height in the heats. Gilbert knew that heats never counted in finals, yet he had no choice. The bar went up another two inches. Gilbert steadied himself, pole in hand. He sprinted down the runway, planted his spike, and soared. He missed, kicking the bar off. He tried a second time. And missed. On his third try, he braced himself, sprinted, planted, and flew. He cleared the bar by a fraction of an inch. But the judges, clearly despising this American who had hacked up their field, had another obstacle. Gilbert had tied, they said, but didn't he want to win on his own? He protested he couldn't go higher without a vaulting box, perhaps the only time in his life he would admit weakness. But he said he'd try. Judges raised the bar not just an inch but another four inches. "Of course, I didn't come anywhere near getting over," he recalled.

Olympic records still list the 1908 pole vault as a tie between A. Gilbert and E. Cooke. Gilbert, however, got the medal; Cooke, recognizing the unfairness, let his friend have the gold. Gilbert took it on a brief tour of Europe. He and a few fellow athletes went to the Alps, where they climbed the Jungfrau, then to Paris, where Gilbert capitalized on his victory. Passing a store that sold bamboo furniture, he asked about bamboo poles of the kind he used for vaulting. He bought fifty for $1.25 each and had them freighted home. On the way back across the Atlantic, he was in no mood for magic, though he won another shuffleboard match and a cup presented to him by Isadora Duncan. Back home, Gilbert sold his bamboo poles for $25 apiece to track clubs around the country, turning a tidy profit of $1,187.50, which he invested in his magic business. But for the boy athlete from Moscow, the money, the medal, even the parade before 200,000 cheering New Yorkers, paled in comparison to the chance to meet his hero.

On August 30, the steamboat *Sagamore* left Manhattan for a sprint across Long Island Sound. On board were seventy-four Olympians. When the boat reached a private dock at Sagamore Bay, the athletes came ashore. Dapper in their dark suits and bow ties, whistling "A Hot Time in the Old Town Tonight," the athletes strode two abreast across a meadow and into the compound of the president of the United States. Teddy Roosevelt, his tank-like bulk filling a white suit, greeted the victors with his bully grin. Here, in the flesh before him, was the manly embodiment of "the strenuous life." "I seldom speak in hyperbole," Roosevelt said in his high, tight voice, "and I want to be taken literally when I say that the feat accomplished by you is one unequalled in the history of athletics. It is the biggest feat ever accomplished by an athletic team." Roosevelt also singled out three "splendid specimens of Oregon manhood," reciting the names Smithson, Kelly, and Gilbert.

That left only the goal of thirteen feet. Although his athletic career was over, Gilbert continued to vault in minor meets. At summer's end, he married the high school sweetheart with billows of chestnut brown hair, the one who, in four years of love letters, he called "my dear little girl." The couple moved into an apartment north of New Haven. In the small yard behind it, Gilbert found enough room to rig a runway, a standard, and a sawdust pit. While starting his magic business and finishing his thesis, "The Genito-Urinary Phenomena of Athletes," he soared in his spare time above the fences of Westville, Connecticut. The following summer, at a small, unofficial meet, he cleared thirteen feet, two inches, an unofficial world record. Then he set aside his pole. President Roosevelt had offered Gilbert and his teammates advice: "Be heroes for ten days, then quit and go to work." So Gilbert went to work, but he never forgot playing what he called "the hatchet man of the Olympics." For the rest of his life, mention of the 1908 games ruffled his customary composure. "Damn it, that's the only time in history that a man was ever allowed to make a record in a heat!" he said more than forty years later. "I always say that I won the Olympics and I don't think anybody who knows the facts will deny that I'm right!"

When it came time to tell boys about his athletic career, Gilbert was modest at first. And for the next few years, surrounded by his own salesmen, a wife, and a daughter, he had little chance to speak to boys in person. Yet like some king craving an heir, Gilbert needed to pass down all he knew. If he could not have his own son, he would raise the entire nation's, or at least raise the bar of their dreams. As he prepared for Erector's second Christmas, Gilbert reached out to boys across the country by starting a "Live Boy's Magazine." Planned as a promotion, *Erector Tips* became much more.

"My object in publishing this boys' paper is to help add to their fun," Gilbert proclaimed in the first issue. "I know what boys like, because I have been a boy myself. My father was always willing that my brothers and I should be given plenty of time for play. I have never forgotten these good times. I want to pass these same good times on to you boys." Despite its title, *Erector Tips* offered few tips on Erector. Each issue displayed readers' models, but as Gilbert promised, the magazine was mostly devoted to "pictures of boys, of the things they do, of magic and tricks they can perform, of huts they can build, and hundreds of other things that boys are naturally interested in." Suddenly, boys who had only a fleeting relationship with other toys developed filial ties to Erector and its inventor. Each month, boys turned to *Erector Tips* for important advice on making billiard balls appear from behind a friend's ear. They learned the virtues of thrift—"How to Save $5.00," and strength—"How to be a Wrestler." They shared their interest in the great war suddenly scorching Europe. "Every one

of us boys likes to hear the guns crack and the cannons roar,"
Gilbert told them. And they shared ideas for weapons of war
made from girders. A sword. A mortar cannon. A battleship. But
above all, on the front page of each issue, they read about a boy
named Bert and his adventures growing up in the Northwest.
Calling himself "The Haymow Athlete," Gilbert eulogized an
American boyhood based on his own. He told boys about the
Red Flag Fire Department, how Bert built the Moscow Athletic
Club, and of the local track meet where Bert won several medals,
a harbinger of things to come. "It was with a vaulting pole that
Bert won the world's championships in the Olympic Games many
years later," the anonymous narrator recounted, informing read-
ers that he "was fortunate enough to go to the same university as
Bert. We had some mighty good times."

Many fathers sharing childhood stories with their sons find
less than open ears. Yet when A. C. Gilbert spoke to them, what
did boys across America do? Did they shout "Back off!" and
slam their bedroom doors? Did they say, "Dad, give it a rest for
once"? No, they responded by writing back. Jack Saxton wrote
to tell Gilbert how he organized his own magic show in
Williamsport, Pennsylvania. Admission was a nickel; box office
receipts totaled 85 cents. The letter closed, "Hoping you are in
good health, I am your little friend, Jack H. Saxton." Some boys
wrote to tell Gilbert of their ingenious uses for Erector. One
made a birdcage for a fallen sparrow. Another built a tank just
like "one of the famous tanks that were used in the great European war by the British in the battle of the Somme." But not
every boy could afford an Erector set. Some could only pay for
the two-cent stamps Gilbert required in exchange for his magazines and catalogs. Among these boys there soon spread a new,
shared sense of longing—Erector envy.

Dear Sir:
    I was looking through these books which you sent me. I
think it is the greatest thing on earth. I am trying with all my
might to get one of these Erectors. Every night I look through

these books which you sent me. I would very much like to have one for Christmas. I have a moving picture machine down here. I am trying very hard to sell it in order to get one of these Erectors. It cost me $8.00 to get one but I am trying to sell it for $5.00. It is in dandy condition, runs by carbide, only used once and all steel, not a bit of tin on it. I would be very glad to exchange it for an Erector but I know you won't do it.

By George, if I had an Erector I would sit up all night and look at it. But the trouble is I haven't got it. Every day I am asking mamma so many questions about the Erector. I am trying to tell her all about the models you can build out of it. But every time the same answer is, if you sell the moving picture machine you can have one. So I am going from house to house trying to sell it. I would be very glad to exchange it. I am very glad you sent me the books. Here I am sending 5 two-cent stamps to get the "tips."

Yours truly,
Arthur Fejesak
Pittsburgh, PA

Bags of letters came from boys in small towns, on farms, in big cities. While Erector made converts coast-to-coast, and later on other continents, in these early days it had its greatest impact in America's industrial heartland. A predominance of letters came from Pennsylvania, Ohio, and Michigan, where sons, imitating their fathers, built their own pint-size machines girder by girder. Some who wrote Gilbert weren't concerned solely with Erector. They were just eager to share their world with the boy named Mr. Gilbert. "Dear Mr. Gilbert: Did you ever have a white rat? I am going to get one in a few days. Signed, Nick." And more than one correspondent, contemplating his box of steel girders, was moved to poetry. H. R. Draves of Freedom, Pennsylvania, wrote,

I surely have had lots of fun
Since my fine Erector come.
Xmas morning, by my bed
There it was upon my sled.

Couldn't wait to don my clothes
As every boy who has one knows
Made one model all complete
Before I even stopped to eat.

I'll not be satisfied, you bet,
Until I own the largest set.
Then from my manual, you'll see,
I'll make them all, from A to Z.

Take Mr. Gilbert by the hand
He's the man to understand
How to make construction boys,
For the "Gilbert" loving boys.

It wasn't Keats, but then, no boys were writing odes to their baseball bats or tin soldiers. Something in Erector had touched a nerve, something more than nuts, bolts, and a motor. The Erector set, it seemed, was also powered by empathy. Other adults constantly pestered boys. Mothers nagged at sons to sit up straight. Fathers told boys to be "seen and not heard." Aunts cleaned nephews' ears with a fingernail, scraping till even a tough boy had to scream and squirrel away. Teachers? Well, teachers. But this man Gilbert understood boys. He knew what it was like to sit in school all day, caged and coiled, waiting minute by minute for the final release at the bell. He knew the feeling of being small in a country that grew taller each year. He shared the hope of making your mark in this world. Building! Exploring! Winning! He knew all about magic and science, toys and tricks, and such practical knowledge as "How to Build a Magic Tight-Rope Walker," a cutout paper figure that balanced on a string. Mr. Gilbert knew what was crackerjack, all right. He knew what was "corking good fun." He knew that Magic Tight-Rope Walkers mattered. And so did Mysterious Handkerchief Vanishers. And starting your own Erector Club! This man Gilbert even knew how to spend a summer vacation. "SCHOOL IS OUT!" Gilbert rejoiced in the June 1915 issue of *Erector Tips*. "I'm as glad as you are—now you can fish, hunt, go on hikes, and spend your vacation having a first class good time. Go to it!"

Fun and empathy won the boys, but they also responded to the good old-fashioned greed aroused by contests. The first two Erector design competitions offered measly $15 top prizes, but in 1915, flush with cash, Gilbert tantalized boys with prizes, prizes, prizes! First prize that year was a car, not some toy model but a full-size, adult automobile. Few states had minimum driving ages, so why not let boys go to it on the road? Gilbert's prize car was a two-seated Trumbull. It was valued at $395, more than a year's wages for some families. Second and third prizes were motorcycles of the Miami brand, retailing for $125 each. The remaining premiums were straight out of All-American boyhood—a canoe, a Daisy air rifle, a bicycle, hockey skates, flashlights, and of course, Erector sets, eighteen top-of-the-line #8s. Boys accustomed to winning some stupid gold badge in some stupid photo contest had never seen prizes like Gilbert's. Meccano, too, had a design contest, gathering about 10,000 annual entries. But in 1915 more than 60,000 letters, each with photos of new Erector designs, poured into the A. C. Gilbert Company.

Among the entries were the usual bridges and battleships, cars and cranes, but as Erector spread to a wider audience, its uses multiplied. Several contest entrants even found a spiritual side to their sets. From simple girders and bolts, one boy in Buffalo, New York, built a twin-spired cathedral modeled after the French basilica at Reims. "We think the boy had been studying the war news and had noticed this beautiful cathedral among the pictures," *Erector Tips* guessed. Several other boys entered churches, but none won a prize. The Trumbull went to a St. Louis boy who bolted together an ingenious replica of the Panama Canal, with locks opened and closed by motor. The following year, Gilbert upped his ante. His 500 prizes included a more expensive car, a Shetland pony ("the best, knowingest pony you ever saw"), and a cornucopia of kid stuff from cameras to fishing rods to camping outfits. But Gilbert knew that prizes alone did not make the boy. An impressionable lad needed a role model, someone who had won something important. After a year of hiding behind the pseudonym "Bert," Gilbert proudly stepped into that role.

Late in 1915, *Erector Tips* featured a five-page article entitled "The Way of a Winner—The Life Story of a Famous Athlete." In those days before Babe Ruth and mass media, famous athletes were few. Shortstop Honus Wagner, the gentlemanly pitcher Christy Mathewson, and "the greatest athlete in the world," Jim Thorpe, were widely admired, but sports celebrity was limited to baseball cards, a cereal box cover, stories told around bars and campfires. Gilbert felt that his athletic feats didn't match those of genuine heroes like Ford and Edison, yet *Erector Tips* presented his story as prologue to the American dream. "Boys! Here is one of the most interesting stories of a real boy you ever read," wrote one "Albert L. Rice." "He was not a great, big, strong boy, but smaller than some of the other fellows. But he wanted to win his first race and he trained to win. He did win and he kept right on winning all through his life—in the grammar school, at high school, at a small university in the northwest, and at Yale. And then, to top off his famous career as an athlete, he won the championship of the world at the Olympic games."

Pictures showed a young Gilbert flexing his muscles in his Idaho backyard, flying over a bar on the field at Yale, and receiving the gold medal from the queen of England. Such success was easy, Gilbert preached. Just follow his path. "I was always interested in athletics from the time I was seven or eight years old," the "Famous Athlete" said. "I love the spirit of competition. It teaches boys to do their very best in everything and to know that they cannot win unless they prepare themselves. It makes them better business men—it teaches them to be square and fair and always alert." Yet in telling his own story, Gilbert was not entirely square and fair. He said nothing of his bitterness at the games, about hacking up the field or tying for the gold. The message,

however, was clear. Boys could be men only if they were first real
boys and real competitors.

Gilbert had reason to gloat, and not just because of his
medals and trophies. At thirty-two, he headed the most successful toy company in history. In 1916 Mysto's sales topped $1.2
million, four times the revenue of any previous toy firm. The
company had sales offices in New York, Chicago, Baltimore, and
Toronto, along with a new plant in New Haven. Gilbert and his
wife had bought their first home and first car. And as if to com-
pensate for the Olympic medal, which Gilbert had lost on his
way back to America, Erector brought home its own gold. The
toy was judged the most outstanding at the 1915 Panama-Pacific
International Exposition held in San Francisco to celebrate the
newly opened canal. With his medal, his magazine, and growing
legions of boys, Gilbert began changing the way toys were sold.
The same year that he topped $1 million in sales, Gilbert started
two new organizations. One, the Toy Manufacturers of America
(TMA), was a genuine organization, and still is. It had a president—
Gilbert himself—an office in Manhattan's Flatiron Building, and
a dual purpose: to shore up industry ethics and promote the sale
of American-made toys. Gilbert's second organization was an institute, but one that existed solely in the minds of young builders.

"Boys, you're always ready for something new and so am I,"
Gilbert announced in time for Christmas that year. "I am just a
big boy myself because I always know just what all healthy, full-
of-life boys want, that's true! I am going to keep on feeling like a
boy, too, and we'll have lots of fun together." His "something
new" was the Gilbert Institute of Erector Engineering, an institute that had no campus, no faculty, and no academic demands.
"In this institute you don't have to do a lot of tiresome studying,"
Gilbert wrote. "You can get all the advantages of it right while
you are playing." Yet Gilbert's institute reached into homes from
Maine to Hawaii. Its members had an average age of about
twelve, and each was fired with enthusiasm kindled by the institute's president. In his pamphlet "How to Become an Erector

Master Engineer," Gilbert boasted, "This is the biggest thing that I ever thought out for you boys."

Gilbert's institute offered a boy three levels of promotion. The entry level was Engineer. To become one, the young designer had to submit a photo of his own Erector model. Younger engineers could make their model with Brik-tor, Gilbert's simplified kit for the "pre-screwdriver set." And each had to assemble the motor in Gilbert's electrical kit. Applicants to the institute's upper levels—Expert Engineer and Master Engineer—had to aim higher. Along with submitting their own models and motors, they had to moonlight as salesmen. Gilbert saw salesmanship as tantamount to triumph. "A boy or man who can sell anything is on his way to success," he told boys. But sales had to be made using "a truthful story." And what could be more truthful than a subscription to *Erector Tips?* To become an Expert Engineer, a boy had to peddle five subscriptions. An Expert also had to submit a teacher's note attesting to his "satisfactory scholarship." A Master Engineer had to sell ten *Erector Tips* subscriptions and submit a teacher's note certifying that he was in the top fifth of his class. For their efforts, institute engineers were handsomely rewarded. Each Erector Engineer received a Diploma of Merit. Experts and Masters earned diplomas plus gold-enameled lapel buttons bearing the institute's name. And Master Engineers went to work for Gilbert, demonstrating Erector sets in stores each Christmas, earning $10 a week plus a 1 percent commission on all sales. A Master also received a personal recommendation from the institute, "indicating that he is the type of boy who is sure to make good."

Like a firm but nurturing father, Gilbert told boys exactly how to achieve his goals. "Say to yourself now: 'Some day I am going to win the highest honors conferred by the Gilbert Institute of Erector Engineering. It isn't easy, but I *know* that I can do it, and I will not stop trying until I succeed.' That's the spirit that wins! That's the determination that has been responsible more than has anything else for the brilliant successes that the world's famous men have made. . . . Think of Edison, Goethals, Roebling, DeForest, Bell, Steinmetz, Tesla, Marconi and Roentgen—all living examples of what boys can accomplish if they start right and are full of ambition and determination."

With encouragement from "The Haymow Athlete" and his eager salesmen, hardware and toy store dealers saw Gilbert's institute as a chance to whip up sales. Many held institute seminars. For one such meeting in Olean, New York, the owner of the Miller Hardware Company rented a local hall. When Gilbert's sales representative arrived that evening, he found boys crowded around the door, clamoring for a seat. The 600-seat hall sold out, and several hundred were turned away. Those who found a seat watched a movie produced by Gilbert's company, and heard a talk by a local boys' club leader. Heading into the night with pamphlets in hand, these budding engineers seemed well on their way to solving their boy problems. And as applications for his institute piled up, Gilbert must have felt the pride of parenthood. For every boy still scrounging the streets, he knew that somewhere there was a boy about to become a Master Engineer—on paper, at least. One of these boys was Harold Heal of Pittston, Pennsylvania.

Boys in Pittston, situated in the heart of the anthracite coal region, didn't have much time to get into trouble. At age ten or eleven, the sons of Slavic, Irish, and Welsh immigrants went to work in the breaker. For nine hours each day, they sat in dim, grimy rooms that roared with the clatter of coal coming down chutes. Their job: pick hunks of useless gray slate from bins of shiny black coal. Pittston was a tough town littered with wooden shanties owned by "the company" and rented to mining families. The Susquehanna River skirting the town ran clear and blue, but the creek alongside the breaker was as black as coal itself. Clotheslines strung between fences were filled with work shirts that never came clean. Up the gradual slope from downtown Pittston stood the two-story clapboard homes owned by the foremen and mechanics who kept the mines running. Harold

Heal was luckier than most boys he knew. He grew up in one of those homes, the son not of an ordinary miner but of a mining engineer. Luther Heal kept an eye on a battery of meters that measured the mine's water and gas levels. He also ran the "cage" that lowered miners from the Glen Alden Coal Company down the shaft each morning and hauled them up each evening.

Harold lived in the middle of Pittston's social ladder, yet it was a shaky ladder at best. He almost didn't make it to adolescence. When he was three, playing in his front yard with a friend, a rabid dog raced down the alley behind the Heal house, leaped the fence, and lunged at Harold. Luther Heal heard the growling and came out of the house. He charged. The dog clamped his jaws on Luther's fist and held on. Luther called for his shotgun. His wife rushed the gun to him, and he shot the dog in the head. For his efforts, Luther got to travel to Philadelphia for weekly rabies shots in the stomach. He also received a Medal for Bravery, with a stipend of $50 awarded by Andrew Carnegie. Having invested so much of himself in his son, Luther decided that $25, an absurd price for any other toy, might make an Erector set a sound investment. A talent for tinkering would keep his son out of the mines, working instead in the machine shop. Harold would make less money "outside"—about $30 a week—but he wouldn't be breathing coal dust all day, coming home with blackened face and lungs, or not coming home at all. Harold got his No. 8 Erector set in 1916 when he turned fourteen.

That November, when he opened his issue of *Erector Tips,* Harold was ready for something new. He had already used his Erector set to make telegraph signal towers and motorized cranes. One day, he even bolted together a doll bed for his younger sister, Florence. Now Mr. Gilbert told him that any boy could earn a degree and a lapel pin. But what design could Harold enter?

Ferris wheels had made their American debut at the 1893 World's Columbian Exposition in Chicago, but they only came to Pittston in the fall at the Luzerne County Fair. So Harold decided to build his own. Bending inch-wide girders into perfect parallel circles, he assembled a Ferris wheel four feet tall, with tiny seats that rocked in baskets as the wheel went around. The model, coupled with the other requirements, made Harold Heal the first Expert Engineer of the Gilbert Institute of Erector Engineering. *Erector Tips* showed Harold in suit and tie, his hair slicked back, his face stern and sober. It wasn't often he had his photo taken. Erector ads also depicted him proudly wearing his lapel pin beneath a headline proclaiming: "Hello Boys! Here's the first ERECTOR EXPERT ENGINEER."

No one knows how Harold celebrated his honor. He did not go on to become an Erector Master Engineer. He may not have played much more with his Erector set at all. Pittston's boys didn't go to high school; they went to work. Harold had written to Gilbert, telling of his "ambition to become an electrical engineer," but shortly after being named an Expert, he began delivering produce in a horse-drawn carriage. Later, needing a living wage to support his own family, he got a job in the mine shop designing machines for extracting and processing coal. In his spare time, he did woodworking, took neighbors without cars on errands in his own vehicle, and helped drive the West Wyoming Nomads, a semipro baseball team, to their games.

Harold worked in the shop of the Glen Alden Coal Company until he died in 1957, just as anthracite mines began closing all over Pennsylvania's Wyoming Valley. He kept his Erector set his entire life, hoping to give it to his sons. When he had two daughters, he held out hope that a grandson might enjoy it, but he didn't live long enough to have grandchildren. He died of a heart embolism a year before his first grandson was born. Harold's diploma did not come from a real institute with a real faculty. The diploma, signed by Gilbert himself, noted that it was an "Honorary Degree." But Harold kept the thin piece of paper until his death. He also saved the copy of *Erector Tips* in which he was featured. No one knows what happened to his lapel pin.

3¹⁄₂

The Chapter That Makes the Delivery Truck

As nearly as I've been able to figure out, my mother threw away my Erector set. Or else she gave it to someone who cared. A junior high science teacher. The son of an engineer across the street. A neighborhood boy destined to be a computer mogul and make us all sorry for what we said. Whatever happened to that box of genuine steel, I never saw it again after about 1963. Yet the more I read about A. C. Gilbert's prizes, his pole vaulting, and his real institute for boys, the more I wanted my Erector set back. I hadn't understood it when I was eight. Born in the time of television, I just didn't have the attention span. Perhaps now, as middle age has given me more yearning than common sense, I might have the patience to build something. Something big. But where in this new millennium would I find an Erector set?

Each summer, the A. C. Gilbert Heritage Society holds its annual meeting. From across the country, members gather to fill a hotel conference room with Gilbert toys. Like collectors' conventions everywhere, the meeting is as much a homecoming as a market. Gilbert enthusiasts talk shop, swap parts, and immerse themselves in the hobby that has filled their attics and spilled into their living rooms, dens, rec rooms, and basements. My first ACGHS meeting was in Dayton, Ohio, a fitting location since it is the ancestral home of those tinkerers extraordinaire, the Wright Brothers. I got to Dayton early, toured the brothers' bicycle shop downtown, then headed for the Ramada Inn on the south side of the city.

Beneath flickering fluorescent lights and a low paneled ceiling, several dozen collectors sat behind tables displaying Erector sets. Others proudly showed off more eclectic Gilbert products— Mysto Magic sets, science kits, and Gilbert Puzzle Parties, those twisted wire puzzles I could never put together without pliers and a crowbar. There were early Erector sets, handsome and stately in their walnut boxes. There were cheap cardboard tube sets like the one I was given. And there were the fantastic sets from the late 1920s—No. 6, "In the Big Red Chest with the Steam Boiler"; No. 7, "The Set That Builds the Steam Shovel"; and No. 9, "Mechanical Wonders Set with 110-Volt Motor"—looking more like giant tool chests than toys. I wondered what they could possibly cost. One price tag was partially hidden by a brass gear. Did it read $95.00? No, it was $9,500. I kept browsing.

Milling through the displays were men my age or older, each with a slight twinkle in his eye. Some merely admired. Others actively shopped, picking up a miter gear here, a two-and-a-half-inch curved girder there, whatever minutiae were needed to turn an incomplete set into a collector's item. Everyone seemed to know everyone else. First names were called out, hands shaken, shoulders clapped in camaraderie as old friends saw each other for the first time since last year's convention. I overheard comments about sets, parts, and Gilbert himself. I envied those able to build almost anything out of Gilbert's invention. In one corner of the room, perched on two tables, sat a twelve-foot model of the *Titanic*, intricately detailed with lifeboats, different decks, windows, and doors, all built from Erector parts. Nearby was a Wright biplane with a five-foot wingspan. Outside was the most incredible model, a six-foot-tall replica of the Palomar Observatory at Mount Wilson. Beneath its curved, sliding dome, its little telescope moved at the touch of a button, while a plastic astronomer sat in a chair. Models like these required more time, patience, and know-how than I could muster if I had been born in the time of Edison. Still, I had to try.

As the weekend progressed, there were speeches, prizes for the best displays, and a banquet of meat and potatoes, coleslaw and rolls. Open houses were held at the homes of local collectors, whose assortments of nearly every Gilbert kit and/or set were carefully laid out in their basements. When I had left for Dayton, friends laughed when I told them I was going to an Erector set convention. And I hadn't expected to have a great time, but I did. I may not have been a boy again, but I had come closer than anything else—old photos, oldies radio stations, having my own boy—had taken me. And I bought an Erector set.

Filled with Erector envy, I returned again and again to the tables holding the 1920s sets. Daring not to touch, I looked at the thick boxes packed with thousands of parts and costing thousands of dollars. Then I looked at my checkbook balance, a meager number that matured me in seconds. I finally found a decent set for a price I could defend. I shelled out $65 for a "Sensational New Erector," the No. 7½ Engineer's Set, with "Reversing Electric Engine and Boiler Parts." The set was made in 1954, the year Gilbert retired from active leadership of his company. Stuffing the rusted red metal box in my suitcase, I headed for the airport. As I passed through the metal detector, I apologized to the security guard for bringing such a blatant box of steel aboard an airplane. "Oh, an Erector set," she said. She opened it, looked beneath the tray of neatly laid out parts, and closed it, waving me on. "I think more kids should play with Erector sets these days," she said. I agreed, unwilling to tell her that in this case, I was the kid.

Home from the convention, I called my five-and-a-half-year-old son over and showed him my Erector set. His eyes widened. He, too, saw the possibilities. Then we opened the manual to decide what to build first. I didn't bother to read him the Personal Message from the Inventor of Erector. I didn't even share Gilbert's advice in capital letters: DON'T TRY TO BUILD THE BIGGEST MODELS FIRST. Boys should build what they wanted to build. But what? The Small Bed? The Mobile Radar Scanner? The Pit Head Gear, which resembled a mine-shaft elevator like the one Harold Heal's father operated? Nate didn't seem to care about any of these. He already had a bed and had never seen the other models in real life. But when I turned the page to a small car labeled "Delivery Truck," we knew we had our first model.

The truck had four large wheels, fenders made of bent girders, a flatbed made from a single perforated plate, and a steering wheel assembled from an axle and a small pulley. The word *cool* hardly did this truck justice. Grabbing a couple of screwdrivers, Nate and I set up shop in our playroom and became builders. It was easy at first. Axles fit perfectly into wheels. Even a kindergartner from the "pre-screwdriver set" could tighten lug nuts to secure the wheels in place. And his father, for whom changing a tire is an existential dilemma, managed to bolt together the girders that became the chassis of the foot-long vehicle. We were sailing along, whistling as we worked. With a turn of the screw, we had the tiny red seat bolted into place. With a twist of a nut, a few short girders became bumper and grille. But then trouble set in, trouble that took me back.

Gilbert had been generous with instructions for his Delivery Truck. Most other designs had only one drawing, but the Delivery Truck was depicted from the side and from a separate "Bottom View." The latter enabled us to see the steering mechanism featuring a gear that turned the front wheels. Or did it? How could it? No way! Despite the "Bottom View," one girder along the floorboard totally hid the steering apparatus from sight, leaving Nate and me to guess. Were we supposed to hook the gear to the axle? To the steering column? How could those two girders fit into that little slot between the grille? Who did this guy Gilbert think we were, anyway? Geniuses? Engineers? Master Engineers?

Nate soon lost interest and wandered off to his Legos. I kept working. I couldn't expect to build something big unless I built something small. After an hour, thanks to this guy Gilbert, I felt even more like a boy. I had all the familiar boyish feelings—frustration, rage, and a creeping sense that I was dumber than anyone else on the block. Above all, I felt righteously pissed off at my Erector set and its lame instructions. But this time I would not quit, nor would I throw my set across the room. My son was watching, after all. Role models, I told myself. Very important in a boy's life. After toiling another hour, I managed to make a reasonable facsimile of the Delivery Truck. It had a seat. It had a flatbed. It had four wheels that rolled. But if you turned the steering wheel, nothing on the vehicle so much as moved. That's because underneath the hood was a steering mechanism that floated free, unencumbered by any gear, girder, or axle. Mine was the only Delivery Truck with a steering wheel that both spun and rotated like an arm in a ball-and-socket joint. Driving it would have been a Mr. Toad's Wild Ride, or the car chase in W. C. Fields's *The Bank Dick*. What Fields said of his own car as he careened around corners would be true of my freewheeling delivery truck: "The resale value of this car is going to be nil."

Feeling sort of proud, I kept my construction in the playroom for a week before I was sure I could take it apart without taking it outside and finding the nearest sledgehammer. Once I had disassembled it, Nate, who by then had built many Lego spaceships far cooler than my truck, never missed his first Erector model.

Having built something small, I leafed through my manual to make my next and, I was sure, final attempt to become the builder I always knew I could be. The Elevated Crane? No, too small. The Windmill Pump? Hey, it was the new millennium. I finally set my sights on a bridge, but not one of those thin, flimsy bridges built with a beginner's set. I would build a genuine lift bridge, about three feet long, to judge by the drawing, with braces, beams, support cables, and a platform that went up and down, powered by my reversing electric engine. If I could build the Lift Bridge, then there was hope. Maybe that first Erector set failure had not been my fault. Perhaps it was never too late to erect an industrious childhood, to be a boy after all. I got a lot of sleep that night and vowed to start on my bridge. Someday soon.

> *Mrs Darling came to the window, for at present she was keeping a sharp eye on Wendy. She told Peter that she had adopted all the other boys, and would like to adopt him also.*
>
> *"Would you send me to school?" he inquired craftily.*
>
> *"Yes."*
>
> *"And then to an office?"*
>
> *"I suppose so."*
>
> *"Soon I should be a man?"*
>
> *"Very soon."*
>
> *"I don't want to go to school and learn solemn things," he told her passionately. "I don't want to be a man."*
>
> —J. M. BARRIE

4

Peter Pan in a Gabardine Suit

On a frigid December day in New Haven, the president of the newly named A. C. Gilbert Company holds his weekly staff meeting. As department heads file into his dimly lit wood-paneled office, a hum and clatter come up the staircase from the factory floor. The noise echoes through the room lined with glass cases displaying the company's toys. Atop the cases sit finished Erector models. On a worktable fronting one wall, unfinished steel structures with girders akimbo make the president's office look like a rich boy's bedroom. One by one, men wearing dark suits and somber faces take their seats at the long table in front of the fireplace. Finally the last arrival sheepishly shuts the door, and the employees sit in muffled silence as the president calls the meeting to order. Through the window, he can gaze into the empty asphalt courtyard below. And like that of a fidgety boy trapped in a classroom, his attention wanders as department heads give their reports.

Sales: "Erector is setting new records, A. C. Applications for the Gilbert Institute are pouring in. Sets are rolling off the line as fast as we can make them. Looks like we might top a million this year!"

New Products: "Our Polar Cub fan did a brisk business last summer, it being so hot and all. The 'big breeze for a little money' sold beyond all expectations. The Erector electrical set is a hit. Wish I could say the same for Brik-tor. More advertising needed, maybe?" The president nods and fingers something in his pocket as he looks out the window.

Engineering: "Following last winter's fire and our recent move from the old Foote Street factory, I'm happy to report that the new plant is back at full production." The president almost smiles but catches himself.

Marketing: "Well, A. C., the year's ad budget—nearly 150 grand, as you may recall—was an unheard-of amount for a toy company. I never thought we'd spend it all. But those two-page spreads you wanted this Christmas ate up every dime. And boys are going crazy over the ads, especially that one with the three kids sitting on the Erector bridge."

Next come reports on personnel, inventory, and plant safety. The president fidgets, rises, and goes to the window, then sits again. The meeting stretches on into late morning. After the reports, the president stands to outline his vision for the company. Competitors keep coming out with the same old gimcracks, he says. Dolls, tin soldiers, the usual windups. A few have tried to capitalize on Erector's success, devising their own construction toys, but they are no threat. Tinker Toys? What boy wants to build with little spools and sticks? Then he grows more somber than usual.

Like it or not, he says, war is coming to this country soon. You can see it in all this talk about "preparedness," the parades, the talk of spies, the suspicion of all things German. And war will mean one thing: the end of toy imports from Germany. The sky will truly be the limit, he says, and that has set him thinking about new products for boys, toys that will teach them all about the world of today's scientists and engineers. "How's the chemistry set coming along?" he asks.

"Ready early next year, A. C.," he is told. "That professor you set us up with has helped a lot."

The president mentions a few other Yale professors who might advise his company on science kits. He imagines Gilbert kits teaching boys about weather forecasting, civil engineering, mineralogy, astronomy, optics, acoustics, hydraulic engineering—there is no end to the exciting things going on in science, and he knows boys will share his interest. Around the table, department heads scribble on notepads and scold themselves for not thinking of these things. Then, a half hour before lunch, the meeting is adjourned. Alone, the president takes off his jacket, trots down the stairs and out into the courtyard in his shirtsleeves and suspenders.

Earlier that fall, when he purchased an empty munitions plant at Blatchley and Peck Streets a few miles north of Yale, Gilbert had planned carefully. The site had ample room for expansion. It was located along the New York, New Haven & Hartford Railroad tracks, saving the company on shipping. And in a quiet neighborhood of two-story cookie-cutter houses shaded by old maples, it was within easy reach of a contented workforce. It also just happened to be—though no one would come out and say this—comfortably removed from the nearest union hall. Yet the new factory lacked one important ingredient—fun. So the president of the A. C. Gilbert Company had a horizontal bar installed out behind the factory, near the tracks. Moments after the morning meeting is finished, though the weather is frigid and his agenda full, Gilbert jogs across the courtyard to the bar for a workout. He begins with chin-ups.

Located along the fault line of World War I, 1916 was among the most sobering years in history. It was as if the new century, born with such promise, had come of age with an attitude. The very notion of Western civilization died that year as unprecedented horrors unfolded in the trenches of France. The Battle of Verdun began that February and lasted until December. Flamethrowers, poison gas, and one-ton shells reduced forests to stumps and men to mere numbers. When winter loomed again, the battle had claimed more than 1 million casualties. Not an inch of ground had been gained or lost. Meanwhile, the Battle of the Somme, with bombardment so shattering it could be heard in England sixty miles away, still haunted modern memory. On July 1, at 7:30 A.M., after seven days of shelling German entrenchments, British soldiers eagerly went "over the top." Scottish troops marched across no-man's-land to the tune of bagpipes. One regiment kicked soccer balls as it advanced. And all were mowed down by machine guns that had hidden deep underground to survive the bombardment. The British suffered 60,000 casualties in a single day. The Somme dragged on another two months, claiming another million men. Spending their third Christmas in the trenches, soldiers believed that the "war to end all wars" would never end. Constant carnage would always be the way of things in Europe. Forever. One German prisoner voiced the despair. "It is the suicide of nations," he said.

America's domestic front, neutral and far from the war, had its own battles. A polio epidemic killed 6,000, a third of them in New York City. More than 2,000 labor strikes broke out across the country. And the United States was invaded. On March 9, nearly 500 soldiers loyal to Mexican insurgent Pancho Villa made a dawn raid on Columbus, New Mexico. Shouting, "Death to the Americans!" they gunned down men and women, burned several buildings, then fled back across the border. What with the invasion, labor unrest, and the end of Western civilization, there was plenty to worry about as 1917 approached. Yet the president of the A. C. Gilbert Company rarely concerned himself with the affairs of the day. *Erector Tips* no longer thrilled to "the guns' crack and the cannons' roar," but Gilbert remained untouched by the doings of adults. That was their world. He was busy building his.

These days, there are many ways to play Peter Pan. Staying "forever young" is a hobby for many an aging adult. Ride a scooter or a mountain bike. Fill your house with "boy toys"— computer games, model trains, old baseball cards. Paste a sticker in your car's rear window that reads "Starfleet Academy." Yet 1916 demanded a more responsible attitude toward growing old. Leisure was not yet an industry, and with toys strictly for kids, most adults were forced to relive childhood through the eyes of their own children. A select few, however, imagined a toyland and went to work building it.

Prolonged adolescence is a label often affixed to men. Men who play harder than they work, men who laugh or whoop only on weekends when the pressure is off, men who enjoy watching other men play games, are said to be just "boys at heart." Gilbert was often so accused. "He's a genius of industry who chose to remain a boy," one associate said. But perpetual boyhood was not Gilbert's choice; it was his calling. Gilbert was no blithe boy. He knew that life was grim, that it had limits. If it was a game, as some said, then it had far more losers than winners. His own boyhood, however, had been boundless. Victory had come easily and often. Even into his twenties, his prowess let him play the same sports he had taken up at ten and keep right on winning. The trophies, the memories, the magic ordained him to preach the virtues of boyhood. If it meant having a dual personality— remaining "Gillie" in his mind while acting as "A. C." on the job—he would somehow pull this rabbit, too, out of his hat. And Gilbert was not alone in his calling. By the 1910s, as the toy business grew, other clever boys were trafficking in their childhoods. While earning respect as titans of their industry, they played all the way to the bank. Yet these grown men found different ways of being both businessman and boy.

The first train Joshua Cohen made nearly killed him. As a boy, he frequently ditched school to play beneath the elevated tracks in upper Manhattan. Cavorting in a cap, playing stickball or one-o'-cat, he could feel in his belly the rumble of trains over-head. At home, he whittled or played with windup trains. The simple toys of the 1880s intrigued Joshua. He once cracked his sister's doll open on the cement steps of his apartment building just to see what made her eyes roll back when she lay down. At seven, he began making his own toys. After whittling locomotives that did little more than roll, he figured out a way to make one run on its own steam. He carved a barrel-shaped chamber, rigged some gears to move wheels, then got some alcohol from a lamp and lit it. The explosion removed most of the kitchen wallpaper, but Joshua survived to play some more. When at sixteen he entered Columbia University to study engineering, he found full-size bridges and buildings boring. He preferred to dream in minia-ture, so he quit school and went to work for the Acme Electric Lamp Company. There he patented a fuse to set off photographic flash powder. The navy heard about it and commissioned the eighteen-year-old to make fuses for mines. Cohen earned a small fortune on the contract, changed his surname to Cowen—in the shadow of Edison, no Jew fit the role of inventor—and started his own business. First he made a small tube with batteries and a light, but grew frustrated by patent suits and gave the rights to his partner. The partner took the little light and founded the Eveready Flashlight Company. Next Cowen made a battery-operated fan. When that didn't sell, he put the motor to a different use as the powerhouse of a toy train that took his middle name—Lionel.

By 1900, toy trains had been chugging around living rooms for decades, but no other toy maker loved them as much as Cowen. And none was such a stickler for detail. Instead of trains that caricatured real ones, he began making flatcars, boxcars, and locomotives that were exact copies, right down to the number of rivets. Instead of wires that tied a train to a battery, he electrified the tracks, wiring transformers that started and stopped a train when they didn't blow a fuse. And instead of growing up, Joshua Lionel Cowen got to play with trains long after other boys had outgrown them. Even as a bald, portly multimillionaire, he still loved his toys. "Marvelous, aren't they?" the seventy-year-old Cowen told visitors to his showroom as Lionel trains chugged through tunnels and across bridges. "They tell me the smoke comes from little pellets you insert in the stacks. Some kind of chemical process. Watch her now as she comes around the curve."

Cowen was more boy than businessman, but Louis Marx had little fondness for boyhood. His own, on the streets of Brooklyn, had been rough, tumbled, and truncated. In 1912, when he was sixteen, his father's tailor shop went broke. Forced to grow up in a hurry, Marx went to work for Ferdinand Strauss, a German toy maker whose windup toys were the most popular toys of their day. Marx soon demonstrated the buttoned-down mind of a ty-coon. Sent to learn the ropes of Strauss's factory, he was running the plant within a few months. At twenty-one, he founded Louis Marx & Co. While Gilbert was tooling his factory to please fu-ture scientists, Marx was making his first killing on Alabama Coon Jiggers. These tap-dancing blackfaced minstrels had been popular since the Civil War, but most toy makers saw them as a tired joke. Marx bought the patent, and during the 1920s, the decade that hosted both the Harlem Renaissance and the resur-gence of the Ku Klux Klan, he sold 8 million Coon Jiggers. Wind 'em up, and the Coon Jiggers danced "an old fashioned planta-tion breakdown." Like Henry Ford, Marx soon mastered the manufacturer's art of making things for less and selling them en masse. During his reign as America's "toy king"—from the Great Depression through the 1960s—three-fourths of Marx's sales came from toys that cost less than five bucks. A tin bulldozer—$1.29. Plastic penguins toddling down a ramp—50 cents. A spaceship—$2. A tin convertible—$2.98. Gilbert must have scoffed, but Marx cared only about volume.

As he aged, Marx came to resemble a clean-shaven Santa Claus, rotund and rosy-cheeked. Yet he was no Peter Pan. Driven to prove himself a grown-up, he took night classes in history and religion at the New School for Social Research. Lunchtime found him jogging in a sweatsuit on the roof of his Fifth Avenue head-quarters while memorizing lists of polysyllabic words culled from the dictionary. Gilbert collected trophies. Joshua Lionel Cowen collected trains. Louis Marx collected generals, numbering among his best friends General Omar Bradley, General George Marshall, and General Dwight Eisenhower.

The clever boy, Joshua Lionel Cowen, turned his hobby into a business. The tycoon, Louis Marx, stumbled into toys as his trade. Which was Gilbert? He was both, but with batteries included. Unlike most members of the new Toy Manufacturers of America, Gilbert had a college degree. This gave him a higher mission than volume or revenue. Louis Marx sneered at educational toys bought only by "hermetically sealed parents who wash their children 1,000 times a day." "Children can learn as they play," he said, "but I don't go along with psychologists who want to sneak up on them and jam education into them through toys." Left to the Marxes and Cowens of the industry, toys would have remained empty-headed fun. Yet Gilbert saw no line between play and learning. He had been an indifferent student, doing his schoolwork only out of duty. Little of it seems to have sunk in. For an Ivy Leaguer, his letters contain an embarrassing number of simple spelling errors—*there* instead of *their, hear* for *here, to* in lieu of *too.* Bored by school, he knew that many boys learned only what they loved, what they built, what they turned over or took apart when no one was looking and no grades were on the line. Throughout his career, Gilbert tried to keep his sets and kits far from schools. "We were afraid that if kids saw our things in school, they'd think they were just as deadly dull as the rest of school and would have nothing to do with them," he said. Gilbert may not have known how to spell, but like Shakespeare's "wise father that knows his own child," he knew boys. And he knew that play could be educational if it toyed with the minds of boys bent on becoming men.

Gilbert's paternal zeal also set him apart. He saw boyhood as more than the sum of its toys, just as his own boyhood had been.

Did he mention the magic shows he used to put on for the neighborhood? Or the time he upstaged Hermann the Great? Gilbert believed all boys should have a similar upbringing. When he talked about his youth, he came alive, telling story after story. Once the stories ended, however, a curious thing happened. He aged before his listener's eyes, becoming somber, reticent, all business. His idol, Teddy Roosevelt, had remained boyish even in the White House. "You must always remember," one of Roosevelt's longtime friends said, "that the president is about six." Gilbert had no such pretensions. The Fountain of Youth that sprang from his ads—"I am just a big boy," "I guess I've never got over being a boy myself"—painted him as a precursor to TV's Mr. Rogers, warmly welcoming boys, getting down on the floor to play with them. But friends found Gilbert about as childlike as your average IRS auditor. He rarely smiled. Executives who worked with him for years said they never saw him laugh. Though he performed an occasional sleight of hand for his grandchildren, he never played with them. "My grandfather and I had a lot in common," said William Chase, son of Gilbert's eldest daughter. "We were both athletes who loved the outdoors, but he never paid much attention to me. At family gatherings he'd always talk to my father. Both were businessmen from the bottom up." And Jeff Gilbert Marsted still wonders why, when he went fishing on his grandfather's estate, the old man fished by himself from an isolated pier. If he wanted Jeff to do something, even if the boy was standing just a few feet away, Gilbert distanced his directive through Jeff's stepfather: "George, tell Jeff to . . ."

The only boyish thing Mary Gilbert saw in her husband was his restless energy. But like wives of her day, she shrugged off his distraction with wry humor. "Why, he hasn't sat still five minutes since he was a baby," she once remarked. "He's always doing something—sometimes several things at once. It's very exciting to be Alfred, you know." Mary likewise knew that to be Alfred was to be awash in angst. Shortly after they were married, when Gilbert was peddling Mysto tricks in New Haven shop windows, his Yale professors came to his new wife. They knew of his plan to become an athletic director, but they hoped to tap her persuasive powers. With his ambidexterity, they told her, Alfred could be one of the world's great surgeons. Couldn't she convince him? Mary rebuffed them. Alfred could never be a doctor, she said. "He would worry himself sick about every patient, and if one of them ever died—which was bound to happen sometime—he could not stand it. I knew what he was like. People are apt to think that because he has so much fun doing almost everything that he doesn't worry. But he is a terrible worrier, especially when he feels responsible about somebody else's life or welfare. So I told the professors I wouldn't try to change his mind at all."

Boyhood may have been Gilbert's calling, but it was also his meal ticket. And making a living at being a boy presented some delicious ironies. He might sit up till midnight forging a new Erector model, but the following day, he had a payroll to meet. Consumed by his business, he never fretted about the creeds that define adults. Politics? During the depression, he openly loathed FDR—a common reaction among corporate presidents—but otherwise he never mentioned affairs of state. Religion? Frank Gilbert raised his sons with daily Bible reading, but once free of this ritual the younger Gilbert never went to church or mentioned God. His wife was a devout member of the United Church of Christ, attending with her children every Sunday, yet the only deity Gilbert seems to have worshiped was Nike, the Greek goddess of victory. Music? Art? Current events? Each was at best a distraction from business and boyhood. These were his two passions, enmeshed in each other like gear and sprocket. And as his company, family, and responsibilities grew, Gilbert used brief boyhood flings like his horizontal bar workout to make adulthood a bit more boyish.

When he came back inside, still puffing from the winter cold, Gilbert often wandered through the noisy factory. As if he weren't company president but just some curious janitor, he walked up and down past rows of workers, greeting them, stopping to ask about their families or their jobs. Huge machinery fascinated him, and amid the constant motion of drive wheels, the musty smell of oil, the slamming of steel on steel, he wandered, marveling at what had grown from his simple idea. His machines turned ordinary steel into dozens of distinct parts. The process was quick and simple. Once cut, bent, and notched, each girder, angle, or slotted strip was coated with grease. Then it was washed in sawdust and tossed into a barrel of churning steel balls that smoothed and cleaned it. After being plunged into a perforated tub suspended in a vat of acid, each part was electroplated in nickel. Finally, the entire assortment was packed in rows and laid neatly in trays, ready to dazzle the first boy who lifted the lid. Gilbert sometimes followed the process from start to finish before his interest flagged. Then, tired from his workout but exhilarated by his factory, he went upstairs for lunch.

After lunch, he worked in his office, but he rarely pored over balance sheets or production figures. Instead he tinkered. Beneath dim lighting, warmed by logs blazing in the fireplace, he devised new models for Erector. One or two constructions could often be found on his desk. He constantly upgraded his sets, making them bigger, bolder, more fun, trying to tap the excitement he'd known as a boy but was finding harder to keep alive as a man.

Under its new motto, "Toys That Are Genuine," the A. C. Gilbert Company made toys that brought adulthood down to size. "Say, boys, here's a new electrical set that's a dandy. A real telephone outfit that you can rig up from your house to the house of your chum and talk to him any time you want to. You can have some corking good times." Once the company name was changed to the A. C. Gilbert Company, Mysto was reserved only for magic sets.

These later sets were not just boxes of tricks. They featured everything a young magician needed to put on a show, just as Gillie had. Each box came with a show curtain, a roll of tickets

ready to sell at the door, and a fake mustache to add an air of mystery. Each also had a poster. All you had to do was fill in your name at the top.

Packaging his past, Gilbert grew older and richer, but he never quite grew up. Yet when he got an idea that might make money, he was all business, quickly filing all the necessary papers for a patent.

Most patents are somber documents protecting better mousetraps and minuscule improvements in machines. Yet U.S. Patent #1,066,809 is the kind only a mother's son could love. Granted July 8, 1913, it is issued to "Alfred C. Gilbert, New Haven, Conn., assignor to the Mysto Mfg. Co., New Haven, Conn." The patent is for "Toy construction-blocks." "This invention relates to an improvement in toy construction blocks, the object being to provide blocks by which toy structures of various kinds may be erected, the blocks simulating what is known as steel construction." In plain English, the patent is for the miniature girder that made Erector "the *only* construction toy with girders exactly like real structural steel." Gilbert often boasted about the flange he invented that night at his kitchen table in 1911. He rarely mentioned his other 179 patents.

Toy building element. Toy motor installation. Toy locomotive. Playhouse. Toy express wagon. Toy gun. Toy vehicle. Toy submarine. . . . But toys were not Gilbert's only inventions. The A. C. Gilbert Company kept track of its patents on typed index cards attributing each to a specific engineer or the boss himself. Among Gilbert's inventions were a fruit-juice extractor, a beverage mixer, an electric drill, an electric fan, a vacuum cleaner (upright), a heater, various switches for small motors, a humidifier, and a vibrator. These products grew out of a decision Gilbert made in 1916. Toys still sold in great numbers only during the Christmas season. This boded a factory that ran like Santa's workshop—full speed from July through December, then idle for six months. Gilbert's workers, however, were not elves. They needed full-time employment. He had already put 100,000 motors in the hands of boys and patented enameled wire to make them run better. Why not put his "motor with a real punch" to work in the kitchen?

In appliances as well as toys, Gilbert proved a visionary. In 1916, kerosene or gas lamps still lit three-fourths of American homes. Kitchens were still hand cranked, heated by firewood, and visited weekly by the ice man. Gilbert, however, had seen the future, and it plugged in. So, a few years before the first affordable refrigerator hit the market, he began making products for the wired home. His first was a $5 portable fan. ("The Polar Cub Electric Fan brings summer comfort within the reach of everyone who lives in an electric-wired house or works in an electric-wired office.") Next Gilbert motorized nineteenth-century tools, making electric erasers, electric pencil sharpeners, electric whisk brooms. Then he went thoroughly modern. By the mid-1920s, the New Haven plant was making mixers, vacuums, hair dryers, and Gilbert's most grown-up device, the personal vibrator.

Hand-held vibrators had been sold over the counter since the late 1880s. Their sexual uses, vaguely suggested but widely known, were hidden behind manufacturers' claims to massage away a variety of medical woes, including fatigue, insomnia, and female "hysteria." In his effort to enter every appliance market, Gilbert designed his own vibrator. Among various patents tucked in his files was a curious document roughly dated to the 1920s. Part Freud, whose theories of sex and the subconscious were then coming into vogue, and part Masters and Johnson (still children at the time), the nine typed pages describe, in candid detail, the Gilbert Vibrator.

"One object of the invention is to provide a means by which

married people can enhance sexual excitement with each other so as to enjoy completion of normal sexual intercourse with the least expenditure of time and energy." The author gives an anatomically correct description of precisely how the vibrator can be used to enhance excitement, then describes how marriages go wrong. "Let us look at the couple whose sexual life is mediocre to drab. The wife or husband does not experience the full and wonderful sensation of completion. And usually it is the wife who is difficult to satisfy. Her entire physical and mental equilibrium is disturbed. Minor arguments arise as is usual when two different personalities are required to live with each other. Each person assumes a defensive state, trying to protect their ideas and 'win the argument.' A so-called mole hill is built up to mountainous proportions. The wife wants the husband to acquiesce to her ideas and visa versa [*sic*]. Both want to win their points. They drift further and further apart. . . ."

Despite the pitfalls of modern marriage, the author knew that some might scoff at a mechanical sex toy, preferring "the good old fashioned way." Yet "if John lived in New York with his wife Mary, and both wanted to go to Philadelphia to a dance, the 'natural way' would be that of walking to Philadelphia." Technology had improved modern life by making cars, so why not use the most modern device in the bedroom?

After clinically detailing the function of glands, the author notes how "every gland acts as a synergist to the other." If one set of glands isn't working right, they all begin malfunctioning. Even the ovaries "may be disturbed. Disuse eventually results in disfunction [*sic*]. This disfunction is eventually manifested by sluggishness and diminution in normal secretion. This lack of secretion results in insidious symptoms. At first they are merely manifested by very slight irritability and possibly insomnia. Then irritability becomes more noticeable. And slowly, they begin to find fault with their close associates—and who is more closely associated than their mate. Eventually, symptoms may subconsciously be transformed into physical ailments. Sex becomes a chore. Every excuse is used to avoid this obligation." The solution, the author claims, is the gadget at hand.

Like many vibrators of its time, the Gilbert device resembled a power drill with an attachment made of bearings, a ball-and-socket joint, and springs. The patented apparatus made a soft rubber disc whir in a gentle massaging motion. Testing this device seems to have made for a hot time in New Haven. The document boasts that "all couples have admitted that their sexual relationships have immeasurably improved. Husbands feel proud of their new ability to thoroughly satisfy their wives. Marital relationships have admittingly become overwhelmingly happy. Small and picuine [*sic*] differences that might often arise are quickly thrust aside. The wife is now extremely happy and content with marital life. The husband is proud of his new prowess."

There is no way of knowing who wrote this unsigned document. When it came time to patent his device, however, Gilbert thought discretion advisable. U.S. Patent #1,668,364, granted in 1928 to Alfred C. Gilbert, was for the "Vibrator," of the type "frequently used by barbers in giving face massages or by physicians and others in the treatment of various diseases, and for other purposes." Gilbert sold his vibrator as the devices have always been sold, with tact. Unable to proclaim "Hello Boys, Make Lots of Orgasms!," he packaged the tool in a box depicting its nonsexual uses—massaging sore hands or feet. The manual inside explained that the vibrator could be used to cure a variety of ailments—rheumatism, indigestion, constipation, headaches, insomnia, nervousness, neuralgia, obesity, bust development ("Do not expect immediate results"), double chin, wrinkles. "Other purposes" were left to the imagination of the long-haired woman on the box cover. Neither Joshua Lionel Cowen nor Louis Marx chose to compete with the A. C. Gilbert Company in making such an adult toy.

By 1916 Frank Gilbert had seen America stretch its legs from the frontier to the industrial age. He had memories of riding in a covered wagon taking him from his birthplace in Michigan to his boyhood home in Indiana. He remembered old men sitting on porches of general stores, whittling and telling stories by the hour. And he recalled how, with his mother dead and his father dying, he had talked his old man into letting him go west. There he married his first cousin, daughter of his uncle Isaac Newton Gilbert. She died just thirteen months later. Frank married Charlotte Hovendon in 1880, and she began to have sons, three in ten years with Alfred in the middle. Almost nothing else is known about A. C. Gilbert's mother. She was there, merely there, for his rambunctious boyhood. "She took it all with calm good humor, and was always there to wipe up the blood and take care of me when necessary," he recalled. His mother remained conspicuous in her absence from every reminiscence he shared with boys. As parental guidance, he mentions only a dad who backed him uncritically. "He encouraged every hobby I ever had," Gilbert noted. "Sports, magic, everything. He and I were regular buddies." But Mom? The only tribute Gilbert ever gave her was in naming his first daughter Charlotte.

In his pocket, Frank Gilbert always carried a small memo book. Its first entry read, "Nothing is advantageous in life that is not honest." The second: "Do whatever you like, but do it to the best of your ability." In his last years as a director of his son's company, Frank Gilbert offered financial advice, but as he approached seventy, he came east less and less often. During one visit to New Haven in late May 1916, he suffered a painful gallstone attack. Rushed to the hospital, he underwent emergency surgery. A week later, he died. His middle son grieved, remembering his buddy with typical stoicism: "Losing him was like losing a part of myself, and I couldn't quite believe he was gone."

Was Frank Gilbert a perfect father? Or did his son's memory, which may have erased his dad's takeover of Mysto, whitewash the usual father-son conflicts? If tension existed between the two, no one ever saw it. Instead, they saw a father who patiently steered his son toward hobbies safer than backyard parachuting and more enduring than bag punching. They saw a dad who cheered fanatically for his son. And they saw a shrewd investor who knew a good business partner when he saw one, having raised that partner to be cautious, clever, and chillingly competitive. "Once or twice a year he came east for a visit to go over the books, to advise about the business," Gilbert remembered. "He was always a great help, too, and I enjoyed every single minute I ever spent with him." Every single minute? Whether gilded by memory or glossed by time, no father could ask for a better epitaph.

While Gilbert was in Oregon laying his father to rest, the new Toy Manufacturers of America elected him its first president. As Christmas approached, 1917 loomed like a bully down the block, but for the president of the A. C. Gilbert Company, adult concerns were tempered by the child within, and one to come. His father was gone, but Mary was pregnant. Sales were surging. Erector Master Engineers were hard at work selling sets in stores across the country. And a whole line of new toys—submarines, machine guns, nurse outfits, and science kits—was in the works. In Erector ads, Dad looked on from a distance, saying, "Hello, boys! Those are some fine models you're making." Now Gilbert looked forward to becoming a father again, perhaps even of a son.

Ten years had passed since he had written Mary from Yale, apologizing for not making it back to Oregon for Christmas. "I don't believe in being in a great hurry to raise a family," he wrote, "but I do want one some day. I realize what a wonderful and kind mother you would be to your children and I think I could be as good as my father has been to me. What great things there are to look forward to in this world for you and I." Now the great things were arriving, one by one. He was right about Mary as a mother. Of his own fatherhood, he was too busy to judge. He might yet turn out to be a Frank Gilbert to his own children, yet in the meantime, a horizontal bar was waiting outside.

On another icy December morning, just before lunch, the Peter Pan in shirtsleeves and suspenders came jogging out of his factory. Arriving at the bar, he blew on his hands and leaped to grab it. Skipping the chin-ups this time, he executed some giant swings, flying in a full-pike position around the flexing bar. He was too stiff to consider a flying dismount, too cautious to try many of his old maneuvers. He was nearly thirty-three now, and the head of a million-dollar toy business. He didn't have as much hair as a decade before, and something had softened the taciturn expression he had worn as an athlete. Was it all those victories? A family? His father's death? As he held himself rigid above the bar, he almost seemed to be smiling. The world hadn't aged him yet. Dropping to the ground, he rubbed his hands together against the cold. Then beneath a thin plume of his own breath, he jogged back inside the factory. His instincts satisfied for a while, he could be an executive for the rest of the day.

5

The Man Who Saved Christmas

When the war came, it threatened to change everything, even Christmas. And Christmas had already changed too much for comfort. Like childhood itself, the holiday was "not what it used to be."

By the time A. C. Gilbert was called upon to save it, our modern commercial Christmas was less than a generation old. Parents told their children about Christmases when all the gifts, each handmade, formed a very small pile under the tree. Gilbert himself recalled childhood Christmases on his uncle's farm, where the extended family gathered, keeping the fire stoked and the festivities flowing. On Christmas Eve, Gilbert parents, grandparents, aunts, and uncles all retired into a parlor. Children could only listen at the door and guess. Was Santa preparing to come down the chimney? Were their parents wrapping gifts—homemade sweets, knitted scarves, perhaps a single store-bought present? Sent to bed with heated bricks wrapped in cloth to keep their feet warm, Gillie and his brothers and cousins did their best to sleep. Then just after dawn, the biggest kid in the house, Frank Gilbert, shouted "Merry Christmas!" and called them all downstairs.

For the Gilberts, as for most families in the 1890s, Christmas was based more on family fun than on giving and getting. By

1917, however, the growing toy industry and its magazine advertising had turned Christmas into the buying season. For those born in the twentieth century, the holiday already meant what it still means to anyone under twelve—toys. And this year, there were more toys than ever. The "Humpty Dumpty Circus." Parker Brothers' Kaleidograph. A miniature Model T that really rolled! Dolls named Flossie Flirt and Baby Bumps. A windup toy that walked like Charlie Chaplin. Erector sets. Lionel trains. These were the child's Christmas currency, and the thought that a war on the far side of a big ocean could stop Santa Claus from making his rounds never disturbed the dreams of Gilbert boys or their sisters. But the war came, promising to consume custom along with calm.

As a thick veil of rain engulfed the Capitol, President Woodrow Wilson addressed a joint session of Congress on April 2. Only six months had passed since the president, campaigning on the slogan "He Kept Us Out of War," had won a cliff-hanger reelection, but the long, brutal winter had destroyed the last shreds of American neutrality. On February 1, German U-boats resumed open warfare in the North Atlantic, sending several American ships to the bottom. Later that month, British intelligence intercepted a telegram revealing a German plot to incite Mexico to war against the United States. Help Germany defeat the gringos, the telegram promised, and Mexican troops could reclaim Arizona, Texas, and New Mexico. Throughout March, Americans itched for a fight. Flags flew as if every day were the Fourth of July. Frantic cheers accompanied "The Star-Spangled Banner" at parades, conventions, and prowar rallies. Pacifists who spoke against the war were dragged from their podiums and beaten. Mobs attacked German immigrants. Some barely escaped with their lives. Some didn't.

Standing before Congress, Wilson called for "a war without hate," one to make the world "safe for democracy." Two days later, while the Senate debated war for thirteen hours, Mary

Gilbert gave birth to her second child, a girl. The couple named her Lucretia. And when the girl was two days old, America joined the Great War, a war that would change everything, even the reluctance of Lucretia Gilbert's father to concern himself with adult affairs.

On a cool, cloudy evening in early June, the Olympia Theater in downtown New Haven was packed. Patrons had come to see a double feature. The first film, *Seven Deadly Sins,* promised to present each of the seven and "what they did to one little girl," but it was the second bill that drew the full house. *The War,* a newsreel, had sold out the Olympia the previous week. Now viewers were urged to "COME EARLY" to see "the brave Tommies leap forth to battle the Prussians—Leviathan Howitzers Hurling Messages of Death—Mighty Battles of Land, Sea, and Air." When the lights went down, ladies removed their hats, as instructed by a slide onscreen. Gentlemen refrained from spitting

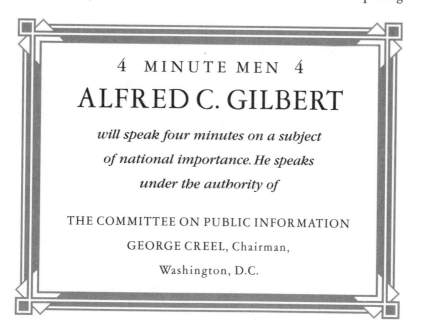

4   MINUTE MEN   4

ALFRED C. GILBERT

will speak four minutes on a subject

of national importance. He speaks

under the authority of

THE COMMITTEE ON PUBLIC INFORMATION

GEORGE CREEL, Chairman,

Washington, D.C.

tobacco juice. The piano player was good, but *The Seven Deadly Sins* proved less lethal than advertised. An intermission followed, with critique of the film. "You call those sins? I've seen more sloth in my living room." After fifteen minutes, cigars burned low; conversations ended with "Well . . ." The houselights flickered, and the audience returned to its seats. But before *The War* could begin, a short, wiry man in a gabardine suit strode onstage. On the screen behind him, a slide explained his presence.

Since joining the debate team at Pacific University, Gilbert had relished all opportunities to speak in public. Whether before a service club, his own employees, or fellow toy makers, he shed his reserve, smiling, telling jokes, performing sleight of hand. But this evening at the Olympia was no time for magic. Standing alone with neither dais nor microphone, Gilbert waited for silence, then began his career as a Four Minute Man.

"Yesterday, nine million American men registered for the draft. Each thus bought a Liberty Bond, and many of them will pay for their bond with their lives. Can we who won't have this opportunity to serve at the front do less than to offer our dollars?" The war would cost America as much in bullion as in blood, he went on. Even after three years of carnage, Germany was determined to fight to the death. "We cannot win this war by waving flags and singing 'The Star-Spangled Banner.' If we want to protect our country and our homes—if we are going to protect democracy all over the world—we must fight, not with cheers and flags and songs but with men and dollars." He recognized that not everyone could afford a war bond, despite the easy payment plan of a dollar or two a week. "But let every one of us who can possibly buy a bond do so and show the country that the men and women and the boys and girls of New Haven are staunch patriots. We cannot all enlist, but most of us can invest. Thank you."

Four minutes went quickly, but Gilbert was under orders to keep it short. He wrapped up his speech to an outpouring of applause. As he entered the lobby, *The War* rumbled onscreen. Gilbert shook hands with the theater owner, then hurried up the

street to the Garden, where the swashbuckling Douglas Fair-
banks was starring in *Flirting with Fate.* He arrived just in time to
address another crowd, then headed home, where Mary was caring for their two-month-old baby, who was not a son.

When the first Liberty Loan campaign ended that June,
Gilbert might have begun staying home nights. But he continued
as one of 25,000 Four Minute Men nationwide. He spoke to audiences on "Why We Are Fighting," "Unmasking German Propaganda," and "Lincoln's Gettysburg Address." Sometimes he
shared the stage with Four Minute Singers performing "When
Johnny Comes Marching Home" or "Pack Up Your Troubles in
Your Old Kit Bag." Gilbert continued to speak throughout the
war; he had never been much of a singer.

As Four Minute Men roused the nation's conscience, the war
made taboos out of all things German. The German language was
banned on streetcars and in high school classrooms. A ham-
burger was nicknamed a "liberty sandwich"; sauerkraut became
"liberty cabbage." And almost overnight, the dolls, circus fig-
urines, and other toys stamped "Made in Germany" vanished
from shelves as if backpalmed by Gilbert's hidden hand. In 1913,
Americans had bought $7,718,000 in German toys, nearly a third
of their total toy purchases. Within two years, German toy imports dropped to less than a million dollars. Once America entered the war, even this sum smacked of treason. As one
newspaper editorial fumed, "To imagine the Hun in the role of
maker of playthings which delight the hearts of children is as in-
congruous as it would be to think of a rattlesnake spitting attar of
roses from its fangs." Gilbert had foreseen this opportunity. He
was not likely to let it pass.

Like manufacturers of steel, iron, and automobiles, Gilbert
retooled his factory. For the next eighteen months, the A. C.
Gilbert Company made parts for machine guns and gas masks.
Under a subcontract from the Winchester Repeating Arms Company in New Haven, the machines that stamped out Erector sets
began making Colt .45s. But with the toy market suddenly free of

German domination, Gilbert made sure that part of his plant kept turning out toys. And as the war effort slowly accelerated, Gilbert began fighting for American playthings. Suddenly he seemed to be everywhere, addressing government councils, Rotary Clubs, and chambers of commerce. While the nation rallied an army, Gilbert organized the Drive of the Big Toy Eight, urging the largest toy makers to produce more than ever for the coming Christmas. That summer, at its convention in Atlantic City, he told the Toy Manufacturers of America that its hour had come. "Germany's old-time prestige in toy manufacture has gone, never to return so far as this country is concerned. If we recognize our opportunity and drive straight ahead . . . there never will be any chance of serious European competition on this side of the water." Mimicking one of his childhood games, Gilbert was playing crack-the-whip with the toy business. Several small toy makers, unable to get raw materials, were whipped too fast and went bankrupt, but those who could hold on were sent flying into the future without a backward glance.

By the time Christmas approached, America had become the biggest toy maker in the world, and the industry had utterly changed. Only four years had passed since Erector had debuted with a modest ad typical of the trade. Now magazines brimmed with jubilant toy ads, many resembling Gilbert's own campaigns. Joshua Lionel Cowen sold his locomotives with a personal approach, signing his name at the bottom of each ad, just like A. C. Gilbert. American Model Builder, the Erector precursor now reeling from Gilbert's success, appealed directly to boys, offering design contests and urging them to think of the "bully fun you'll have." Winchester rifles aped Gilbert's institute, encouraging boys with .22s to compete for a gold medal as "sharpshooter" or a silver one as "marksman." Yet for all its commercial trimmings, Christmas during the war was haunted by a most unseasonable emotion—guilt.

Self-denial, Americans were told, was the key to defeating the Huns. People were told to eat less so they could send more food to hungry Allies. They were told to buy less, the better to purchase Liberty Bonds. Patriots observed Meatless Mondays, Wheatless Wednesdays, and Porkless Thursdays and Saturdays. They ate coarse, dark "Victory Bread," made with whole wheat that wasted less grain. Sugar was strictly rationed. Peach pits were collected in public barrels, to be made into a charcoal powder used in gas masks in the trenches. With sacrifice as the season's leitmotif, how could parents enjoy spoiling their children with toys? Shouldn't they keep Christmas as simple as the holidays they cherished from childhood?

Gilbert saw the problem coming and had an answer: "Don't Cheat Your Boy on Christmas Morning." In full-page ads beneath this headline, he shared one mother's concerns. Seems her son was dismantling everything in the house—the clocks, the phonograph, the washing machine. "I don't know what I'm going to do with my boy," the mother moaned. "He's getting so *destructive.*" This mother, Gilbert announced, was "*cheating* her boy—yes, cheating the lad's creative instinct." The poor youngster only wanted to take things apart, yet his parents had given him just carts, balls, and games—"useful and necessary, of course, but not enough." There was only one solution, though it came in several sizes. But on beyond Erector, Gilbert sought to soothe parental guilt. For this "first real War Christmas," parents should resist any temptation to cut back on presents. "The little folks—that boy who'll be the boy in khaki, if such are needed in a few years—that boy who has so few childhood Christmases at best— tell me, honest now, is it right to sacrifice him? Should that little chap of yours, who's dreaming even now of Christmas morning, be forgotten, disappointed on that day of all days for a boy? Sacrifice the big folks' Christmas if need be, but as long as we can, let the boys and girls have Christmas!"

And so they did. The growing pile of presents under the tree that season included lots more Gilbert toys. For the first and last time he made war toys, including the Gilbert Crushing Tank, Gilbert Machine Guns that fired cork bullets, and a nurse's outfit for girls. Also out in time for Christmas was the Gilbert chemistry set. Porter Chemical had sold its Chemcraft sets since 1914, but Gilbert ads quickly gave chemistry his own personal touch: "Have you ever seen an egg inside a narrow necked bottle and wondered how it got there? I have, lots of times." The ad didn't reveal where Gilbert had seen such a marvel, yet it was not vague about the value of chemistry, "the most important of the sciences at present." Doubting Toms, Dicks, and Harrys were told to look around them. Ink, soap, leather, batteries, even their daily meals, were made or enhanced through chemistry. And when soldiers in the trenches choked on phosgene or mustard gas, why that, too, was chemistry! "We all know of the part it is playing in the European war," his first chemistry manual noted. "Indeed, it has been stated that Chemistry is the greatest weapon of the conflict. We have read of the use of liquid fire, poisonous gases, high explosives—all of these come within the realm of Chemistry."

So what trouble could a Gilbert chemistry set cook up? Homemade TNT? A way to turn "liberty cabbage" into a stink bomb? Sorry, boys, but Gilbert played it safe. Young chemists could test for acids and bases with litmus paper. They could make ammonia, soap, ink, rock candy, or shaving cream. They might electroplate objects with nickel or copper, manufacture white lead, or "petrify" a little sister's baby shoes. And as promised, they could insert a hard-boiled egg into the mouth of a bottle. A lit match inside sucked the egg right in. Chemistry was "the grandest, oldest science of all," Gilbert assured boys, yet the former magician couldn't resist throwing a little hocus-pocus into the mix. Unlike Chemcraft, each Gilbert set included a "Magic Program—With Patter Talk."

Christmas evening, 1917: Dinner is done. The family is sharing stories, breaking out the brandy. From the bedroom steps a lone chemist-cum-magician, about ten years old. Even though it's Tuesday evening, he is wearing his Sunday coat and tie. He taps a wand on a glass. "Ladies and gentlemen, boys and girls! May I present a little magic for your amusement this Christmas?" Slowly the talk dies down. The lights on the tree flicker.

"Battery must be low," Father says. He stands to check it, but Mother calls him back with a hand and a whisper.

"You should watch," she says. "He's been practicing all afternoon in his room."

"I thought you bought him the chemistry set, not the magic set."

"I did. It cost $4.75."

"You could have bought a Liberty Bond."

"I know, but he wanted—"

"Ladies and gentlemen," the boy almost shouts. "I am going to perform for you tonight a series of experiments in scientific leg— leger— legerde— something or other. Anyway, I am going to demonstrate to you that there are around us everywhere natural spirits, and possessing the ability to call up and make use of these natural spirits, I shall give you the pleasure of seeing mysteries of another world." The boy then sets a glass of water on the table. After taking a sip, he holds his wand aloft. As the family watches, the chemist waves his wand over the glass. Instantly the water turns the color of burgundy. Gasps pass through the dining room.

"Amazing!"

"Incredible!"

"How did he do it?"

"And your brother always says our boy is such a chump!"

How did he do it? (Hint #1: When a passing wand drops a few crystals of potassium permanganate in water, the liquid turns the color of wine.) But there is more.

"Now, ladies and gentlemen, before I prevail further upon the powers that be, I want to have you know that everything you see changed has assumed a new form. I do not stoop to substitution by sleight of hand. For example, I have here a glass of wine. By passing my hand over it thus, I change it to back to water. If you do not believe it is possible, watch closely." The boy waves his bare hand slowly in front of the glass, and . . . the color disappears! It's ordinary water again, though this time he doesn't drink it. What kind of chemistry set is this? (Hint #2: The kind that includes hydrogen peroxide, a few drops of which, sprinkled in water, bleach the potassium permanganate and make the water clear again. Science marches on.)

The family bursts into applause. The Christmas lights dim again, and Father starts to rise. But wait! There is still more. "For my next magical trick, I will pour milk from a bottle full of water. Watch carefully now!" Before the curtain comes down—or is dragged down by Father—the boy has poured milk from his water bottle. He has blown the color out of a blue handkerchief. He has written his name, then blown it off a piece of paper. And he has become a Gilbert boy, an odds-on favorite to write a letter or send a poem to the man who understands him better than the leaders of any chemical company. Whether the boy will grow up to be a chemist or a magician remains a mystery, though with Houdini now passé, chemistry is the better career move.

A decade after the Gilbert chemistry set hit the market, Yale professor Robert Treat Johnson was surprised by a sudden upsurge in enrollment for his chemistry courses. Johnson polled classes and found that more than half his students had been inspired by a Gilbert chemistry set. By the time the first generation of Gilbert boys began careers, Gilbert was receiving nearly 1,000 letters a day, but he proudly singled out those that came from big boys. "I thought you might be interested in knowing what happened to one of the kids who 'cut his teeth' on a Gilbert Chemistry set," one began, "so I am enclosing a reprint of a paper titled 'Determination of Oxygen in Titanium,' which I presented at the last meeting of the American Chemical Society." Other Gilbert science kits would come and go, but the chemistry set remained a top seller until 1967, when the A. C. Gilbert Company itself disappeared as if it had been blown off a sheet of paper.

Declaring war had been easy, but getting an American army "over there" took the better part of a year. By Christmas, only 175,000 Yanks were in France, but the enemy could almost hear millions more marching. Throughout the spring of 1918, German soldiers hurled themselves against Allied lines in a desperate attempt to force a surrender before the Americans arrived. In mid-March, they punched a hole in British defenses near St. Quentin. Suddenly they could imagine their way to Paris, just sixty miles off. Yet exhausted Allied forces rallied. From Reims in the south to Ypres in the north, the German advance bogged down in muddy shell holes from previous battles. Then, the thing Fritz and his company most feared came to pass. A year after Wilson went to war, American troops in their tin-pan helmets began pouring into the trenches. Under the slogan "Lafayette, We Are Here," a quarter million Americans arrived in France in May. The following month, 278,000 came. In July, from flag-strewn docks in Hoboken, Newport News, Boston, and Philadelphia, another 300,000 boarded what they called "the Atlantic Ferry." Disembarking in France, they readied themselves to turn the tide. Back home, families received word that their sons had fallen at Château-Thierry or Belleau Wood. For the next four months, neither all the Gilbert Crushing Tanks nor all the boys marching with their Gilbert Machine Guns could stop the war from taking its toll.

Making patriots out of ordinary citizens was the job of the Four Minute Men, but doing the same for manufacturers fell to the Council of National Defense. The council met weekly to discuss war production. Industry by industry, tight-lipped businessmen were summoned to Washington, D.C., to meet in the office of the secretary of war. There they discussed what they could do to help our boys overseas. Before the austere council, coal tycoons fixed their prices at $3 a ton. Oil barons agreed to stockpile strategic reserves. Manufacturers griped and groaned but knuckled under to wartime demands that cut prices, increased paperwork, and still made them vastly richer. Leaders of every major industry met with the Council of National Defense. Eventually, even toy makers had their turn.

Secretary of War Newton D. Baker was one of those men who seem never to have been a boy. Slight of stature, with wire-rimmed glasses and a studious demeanor, the young Baker did not spend his youth staging tricycle races or honing his skill with Indian clubs. Instead, he read. But while other bookworms pored over *Treasure Island* or *Tom Sawyer*, Baker's favorite bedtime reading was *History of the Intellectual Development of Europe*. Instead of earning medals in hometown track meets, the young Baker earned a prize for plowing through the entire *Encyclopaedia Britannica*, from *Aa* to *Zwingli*. Growing up to be a lawyer and a skilled orator, Baker became Cleveland's "big little mayor" when he was just forty. When his term ended, President Wilson summoned him to Washington, D.C., to take over the War Department. Baker balked. He was a pacifist, he told Wilson. He "had never even played with tin soldiers." Very well, Wilson said. "Are you ready to be sworn in?" Republicans mocked the 125-pound Baker as "Newtie Cootie," but he adroitly managed the nation's war needs, raising an army of 4 million in just eighteen months. Zealous in his insistence that the entire nation rally to the war effort, Baker sat stiffly in his chair late on a September afternoon in 1918, preparing for a meeting with a group of toy manufacturers.

With the war going well but still requiring steady sacrifice, the representatives of the Toy Manufacturers of America had been allotted fifteen minutes at the end of the council's busy day. Like spokesmen for other industries, toy makers deserved a chance to explain why theirs was a vital commodity without which victory was impossible. Newton Baker and his men, not trusting parents to cheat their boys this Christmas, wanted to cheat all the nation's children out of gifts. The council had proposed a ban on all toy sales for the 1918 holiday season. When the ban was suggested, Gilbert had just finished his two-year term as TMA president. No longer the trade group's spokesman, Gilbert nonetheless knew a Scrooge when he saw one. Alarmed by the council's impending ban, he asked for a hearing, then hastily gathered fellow toy makers and headed to the Navy Building in Washington, D.C., for a showdown.

Evening was descending, but the sweltering heat of summer hung over the capital as Gilbert and his fellow toy makers entered the Navy Building and were briskly searched. Guards opened their packages and puzzled over the contents. A toy steam engine? A small submarine? Wire puzzles? Boxes of slim steel strips? The guards were suspicious until Gilbert told them the group's name. Then, with bundles repacked, the visitors were allowed to enter. Their footsteps echoed as they moved down the marble halls and into Baker's office. As befitting the War Department, the high-ceilinged room was solemn, shaded by drab drapes and flanked by stiff leather davenports. Behind a table littered with inkstands and quill pens hung three large portraits of starched men in starched suits. Around the table, the council finished up old business.

Only four of the six council members considered toys even worth the trouble of showing up. Baker sat in the middle, one leg tucked under him, the other dangling freely but not reaching the floor. As the toy makers prepared their presentation, he peered through his glasses at papers in front of him, editing his agenda for the rest of his fifteen-hour day. On his right sat Secretary of the Navy Josephus Daniels. The very opposite of Baker, Daniels was boisterous and flamboyant. A former newspaper editor from North Carolina, he was known for rambling speeches filled with old jokes, poetry, and biblical quotations. Daniels had been the last of Wilson's cabinet to agree to war, nodding his acceptance with tears in his eyes. For this afternoon's meeting, he wore a white suit, a bow tie, and a smirk beneath his expanding forehead. Toys? Essential to the nation's war effort? Next thing you knew, the hot dog makers would be coming in here trailing strings of sausages "our boys must have in boot camp."

On Baker's left sat another man who seemed to have leaped straight from crib to college. Bald, plump, and straitlaced, Franklin Lane seemed the very model of a governmental pen pusher. A Canadian by birth, Lane had moved as a child to California's Napa Valley, arriving there wearing the kilts of his native Prince Edward Island. He had gone to work at age eleven, as a messenger boy, then climbed his way into the University of California. First as journalist, later as lawyer, Lane preached the patriotism common to self-made men. During Cabinet meetings, the president often cut short Lane's jingoistic tirades. It had been Lane's idea as secretary of the interior to have leaders of industry meet with the Council of National Defense. After the war, although the council had done nothing but recommend this or that, he called it "no doubt the greatest organization of its kind that the world has ever known." Ahem.

Rounding out the afternoon's attendance was the council's Wall Street mogul in residence. Bespectacled and balding, with a bushy red mustache, William Redfield looked more like Daddy Warbucks than a secretary of commerce. "Toys?" his expression huffed as he nervously parted his luxuriant mustache with fingers and thumb. "This must be some kind of joke."

These were the men in whose hands the coming Christmas rested. These were the men Gilbert had warned boys about in *Erector Tips* when he wrote, "I've noticed that men who looked as though they never had any fun when they were boys, and who have no boys of their own, are the kind of men who chase the boys out of their yards and swear at them, who complain to the policeman about the boys playing in the street near their houses, who keep your baseball and football when it goes in their yards and try in every way to spoil your fun." With the stroke of a pen, these men had the power to spoil boys', girls', and Gilbert's own fun. And as Gilbert put his bundles behind a davenport and stepped before the men, he saw they had every intention of upholding their Dickensian plan.

Every other segment of society was sacrificing for the war effort, the council reasoned. Why not children? Weren't kids already giving speeches as Junior Four Minute Men? Didn't government bulletins sent to schools lecture kids about patriotic sacrifice, telling them, "If you have your shoes patched and wear them longer, you are helping to win the war. If you take good care of your clothes, you are saving just as surely as one who has money to buy stamps. If you sift the ashes and save coal you are helping. If you clean your plate at the table that will help." So why not ban toy sales and encourage parents to put Liberty Bonds in stockings instead?

With his toys tucked away, Gilbert began his prepared speech. Despite his gold medal and world records, it is doubtful that any council members had heard of him. To them, he was just another desperate manufacturer seeking to shirk wartime belt-tightening. Still, they had to admit, he spoke with the brevity and conviction of a Four Minute Man. He began with statistics: Total sales. Domestic revenues. Imports. Tariffs. Then he turned to the subject he knew best. "The greatest influence in the life of a boy is his toys. A boy wants fun, not education. Yet through the kind of toys that American toy manufacturers are turning out, he gets both. The American boy is a genuine boy and he wants genuine toys. He wants guns that really shoot, and that is why we have given him air rifles from the time he was big enough to hold them. It is because of the toys they had in childhood that the American soldiers are the best marksmen on the battlefields of France."

A murmur passed through the council. Was it agreement? Resistance? A thought of dinner? Gilbert continued. "America is the home of toys that educate as well as amuse, that visualize to the boy his future occupations, that start him on the road to construction and not destruction, that as fully as public schools or Boy Scout systems, exert the sort of influences that go to form right ideals and solid American character." Gilbert spoke for ten minutes. Toys were not mere playthings, he said. They were the blueprints of future men and women who would fight wars and

preserve the peace. Deprive youngsters of toys, especially educational toys, and "the country will lose a generation of doctors,
engineers, and scientists."

Years later, Gilbert would recall the occasion with typical
platitudes. It was, he noted, "one of the happiest and most successful undertakings I ever participated in. I was earnest, I was
honest, and I was sincere. I had a real story to tell, and I had the
toys to prove my point." And after proving his point with words,
Gilbert turned to other toy makers for a brief consultation. The
men agreed that these stick-in-the-muds seemed to be loosening
up. The secretary of war had twice adjusted his glasses. The secretary of commerce had stopped scribbling on his little pad.
Apropos of nothing, a wry smile had appeared on the secretary of
the navy's face. With Gilbert's speech finished, everyone knew
there was little more to be said and little time left. Maybe they
should bring out the toys. So, from behind the davenport came
bundles that were quickly unpacked and set on the table.

Within seconds, the Council of National Defense dropped its
guard. The toys turned into time machines, and the bureaucrats
turned into boys. Like kids making their first visit to FAO
Schwarz, they marveled and played, reached and grabbed. Each
man locked onto a favorite and wouldn't let go. While Newton
Baker watched in amazement, his colleagues rose from their
chairs and sat down on the floor to play. The secretary of the
navy picked up a toy submarine. He turned it over, noting the
torpedo holes, raising the periscope, imagining a German U-boat
in his sights. Suddenly self-conscious, the Honorable Josephus
Daniels looked up from his compromising position on the carpet.
Striving to appear secretarial, he asked, "Are such submarines on
sale throughout the country?" Gilbert assured him that they
were. The secretary nodded and turned back to his sub. "There's
no use trying to deny the toys get every one of us," he said.

On the far end of the floor, the secretary of commerce sat ex-
amining a toy steam engine. Ever interested in power, industrial
or financial, William Redfield tinkered with the machine's valves

and peered into its boiler. Finally, he asked how to start the damnable thing. As it chugged and churned, the secretary brushed at his whiskers and blustered, "I learned the rudiments of engineering on an engine like this." Back at the table, Interior Secretary Lane had found a children's book on aviation. With a contented smile, he skimmed through its pages, then asked politely where he could get more books like it.

Well beyond the allotted fifteen minutes, the Council of National Defense amused itself with its toys. The Cabinet officers played with wire puzzles, tin soldiers, and other toys they had considered keeping out of the hands of children. Then, regaining their composure, they set the toys aside and conferred with the secretary of war. Baker had once boasted to Daniels of his stubbornness. "I am glad if anybody can convince me that I am wrong," "Newtie Cootie" said to the secretary of the navy, "but I am damn sure that nobody lives who can do it." Yet now he fell under the suasion of the rest of his council, each of whom had just been visited by the Ghost of Christmas Past. While Gilbert and his group waited, the bureaucrats mumbled.

Toys, they agreed, *did* assemble children as much as vice versa.

Perhaps they *were* essential to a wartime economy.

It couldn't hurt—

No one knew how long the war—

And so, the Council of National Defense changed its mind. There would be no ban on toy sales that Christmas, Baker announced. Gilbert thanked the men for their time. The council thanked him. Then in lockstep with his colleagues, Gilbert left the toys with their new owners and trudged down the echoing halls of the Navy Building and out into the evening.

Back in New Haven several weeks later, Gilbert was in his office when his secretary informed him that a newspaper reporter was on the phone. The *Boston Post*, America's largest-circulation daily newspaper, had heard about the meeting and wanted to do an article. Gilbert hesitated. Like many businessmen, he was suspicious of any publicity he could not craft himself. Other than a short item in the *Wall Street Journal* the previous January noting his sudden success, his name had not been in the papers since it had appeared beneath pictures of him soaring on the end of a pole. He agreed to a brief interview, on one condition. The reporter must note in the article that *he* hadn't changed the council's mind—the toys had. The *Post* correspondent took the train to New Haven and caught a cab to Blatchley and Peck Streets. On the third floor of the factory, he found Gilbert in his office with a fire going. Before he could ask a single question, the reporter was charmed by the office itself, which he described as "a fascinating place, with great cabinets all full of toys, and the walls all covered with the athletic trophies and awards from Olympian games." Then, Gilbert told the whole story. On October 25, the *Post* headline read,

CABINET MEMBERS BECOME BOYS AGAIN

Describing the council meeting, the reporter saw it through the eyes of America's youth. "How the boys and girls of America would have laughed if they could only have been concealed in that room and, peeking over the tops of the davenports, seen the Cabinet playing with the toys!" A photo caught Gilbert in profile, stern-jawed and serious beside an Erector set, a Crushing Tank, and an airplane. The caption hailed him as "THE MAN WHO SAVED CHRISTMAS FOR THE CHILDREN." "Remember," Gilbert warned the reporter, who closed his story with the quote, "I didn't do it. Tell them it was their own toys that won the day!"

As the war ground to a close, all of Gilbert's wartime efforts paid off. A few days after the *Post* article appeared, the Dutch merchant ship *Nieuw Amsterdam* sailed into New York Harbor with a long-overdue cargo. The ship had been sitting in Rotterdam since the beginning of the war, pending consent of the U.S. State Department to import the cargo and a German guarantee that it would not be torpedoed. After four years of waiting, the *Nieuw Amsterdam* received both agreements. In October 1918, it crossed the Atlantic. In its cargo holds were 4,000 cases of German toys valued at $250,000. Some speculated that this ship was sent see whether Americans were still interested in toys made by Huns. If so, the toys failed the test. The German toy ship made news around the country. Editorials, women's clubs, and groups of "War Mothers" denounced the very idea of German toys. The American Defense Society urged mothers to examine toys carefully for the label "Made in Germany" to "show Germany that goods made by her bloody-handed baby-killers will not be tolerated in America."

As the *Nieuw Amsterdam* sat in port, Gilbert was in Manhattan's Flatiron Building chairing a meeting of the TMA's War Services Committee. Learning of the cargo, the committee quickly urged a congressional ban on German toys until an armistice was signed. But Gilbert and his peers did not need such a ban. Their own toys had been noticed. "American toy-manufacturers have stript [*sic*] us of the last vestige of an excuse for the purchase of toys from the Huns," a hardware trade journal noted. "Our factories are making more toys than we ever imported, and they are not the flimsy jim-cracks we formerly bought from abroad. They are largely exercise toys which develop a child's body, or mechanical or structural toys which train the mind. Before the war we imported eight million dollars' worth of toys from the Central Powers. Who will make our kiddies' toys in the days to come? Once more, Mr. Buyer, it's up to you."

A few days after the *Nieuw Amsterdam* was sent home, on the eleventh day of the eleventh month at 11:00 A.M., the war ended. Across Europe and America, spontaneous celebrations began. In New Haven, where the news arrived at 5:00 A.M., there was predawn dancing in the streets. Later that morning, an impromptu parade, to the tune of bells, whistles, and guns, marched through downtown. Cheering crowds carried effigies of the kaiser hanged, caged, or handcuffed. The war was over! In December, as parents boosted toy sales even further, Gilbert received a Four Minute Man certificate signed by the president. He stored it with his membership cards from the New Haven Yacht Club, the Connecticut Automobile Association, and the Society of American Magicians. The following year, diplomacy would sow the seeds of the next war. In the meantime, "the man who saved Christmas" had made sure that genuine American boys and girls would not be cheated that season or any other soon to come.

> *When I was a little girl, I wished I was a boy.*
> *I tagged along behind the gang and wore me corduroys.*
> *Everybody said I only did it to annoy,*
> *But I was gonna be an engineer.*
>
> *Mama told me, "Can't you be a la-dy?*
> *Your duty is to make me the mother of a pearl.*
> *Wait until you're older, dear, and may-be*
> *You'll be glad that you're a girl."*
> —PEGGY SEEGER

6

The Girl Problem

Though it may have missed a few, the 1920 census counted 17 million American girls under the age of fifteen. Combined with a roughly equal number of boys, this slice of youth was the largest piece of the American pie. Seventeen million is a number that thumbs its nose at generalization, but if the flappers of the era are any litmus test, this was a new breed of girl. Few toiled long hours in factories. Fewer still bound their bodies with corsets or corseted their minds with Victorian morals. A girl of the 1920s had better things to do, and more time in which to do them. More than a million now went to high school, and many could even look forward to college. They were not yet, as F. Scott Fitzgerald would write of their older sisters, "accustomed to be kissed," yet they could easily imagine being so. A girl raised in the 1920s looked forward to unprecedented possibility. After seventy-two years of marches and arrests, women had won the right to vote. Pioneers like Congresswoman Jeanette Rankin and anthropologist Margaret Mead were marching into male domains. A girl could not yet be anything she wanted, but she could dream, couldn't she? And regardless of her dreams, each of the 17 million American girls had one thing in common. She was rudely ignored by the nation's leading toy maker.

"Hello Boys! Make Lots of Toys!" "Boys, it does my heart good to read some of your fine letters." "Yes, boys, I've been one and I know what makes a hit with boys." "Boys, if you ever have a chance to go to college, do so, because . . ." "Be an electrical wizard, boys!" "Are you one of those boys who has hesitated to take up wireless operating because you think it is too complicated?" "Yours for fun, boys, A. C. Gilbert." Boys, boys, boys. It was enough to drive a girl crazy, if she let it.

Growing up in the late 1920s, Elaine Grotefeld liked putting things together and taking them apart. On the leafy streets of Lakeview, North Chicago's predominantly German section, Elaine was known as the tomboy type. She played with dolls, including the most popular on the block, Raggedy Ann, but she preferred hammering nails in her father's basement workshop, playing King of the Hill, and "doing all kinds of things boys mostly were doing." She owned her neighborhood's only baseball and bat, making her welcome in any alley game. Short and freckled, with straight brown hair, Elaine cut a tomboyish figure. Her father, Harold, a purchasing agent for Westinghouse, tolerated his daughter's tendencies; her mother even condoned them. "My mother was quite a feminist for her time," Elaine recalled. "She felt girls were denied too much." Yet when their daughter cast her eyes on an Erector set, that was going too far.

Nearly seventy years later Elaine recalled, with only a hint of irony, the "painful memory." At Christmas in 1933, Chicago was in the grip of a cold wave, with temperatures dropping to single digits. The depression, not yet bottomed out, made each house a bleak one, each sky whiter, each building more gray, as if life itself were a movie shot in black and white. Since spring, the new president's Fireside Chats had fostered hope, but a quarter of the nation was still unemployed. Bread lines were long, and the

Grotefelds were determined to avoid them. Escaping the city for the holidays, Elaine's family celebrated that Christmas at her grandmother Lindgren's house in Evanston. Due to the hard times, Elaine's five-year-old cousin Larry and his parents were boarding in the huge old two-story house. Two roomers paying rent to keep the family afloat were also on hand for the holiday.

The depression had hit the Grotefelds no harder than other families, but children could see the toll written on the face of every adult. Elaine's father had lost his job at Westinghouse and was just getting by as a freelance hardware salesman, working strictly on commission. Larry's father had also been laid off. So when eighteen family members gathered on Christmas Eve, the celebration was of the kind meant to mask tough times, not culogize good ones. Toasts were humble and reverent, frolicking subdued. The air hung heavy with the smells of Old World cooking. The Swedish side of the family had prepared a smorgasbord complete with meatballs, potatoes, beets, and warm, freshly baked bread. And there was plenty of glögg, a Scandinavian punch of wine brewed with cinnamon, cloves, raisins, and orange peel, spiked with any store-bought liquor on hand, then sugared and served piping hot.

After dinner came the usual carols and desserts. Then as snow began to fall outside, the family turned to the gifts under the tree, which stood taller than anyone in the living room. Aunts and uncles, older nieces and nephews, each opened presents, showering thanks on each other for small favors. And then, after the children had opened a gift or two, only one remained under the tree. "It's for you, Larry," Elaine's cousin was told. Larry tried to lift the package, but it landed on the rug with a heavy clank. When his father hefted it, the present clattered like some Model T engine past its prime. With a knowing smile, his father set it down in front of the boy. Larry wasn't sure if he should open it or slowly back away. "Open it!" several urged. Tearing off ribbon and wrapping, Larry found something that made all his tin soldiers look like last century's toys.

Not many families could afford a $20 toy that Christmas, unless they had a dealer's discount, but Larry and Elaine's grandfather owned Lindgren Wholesale Electric. Business had been bleak. Construction had dropped to zero. Contractors were lining up at soup kitchens, not wholesale dealers, and Oscar Lindgren had to squeak by on his retail business. Along with the latest Gilbert gadgets—blenders, hair dryers, and mixers—Lindgren Wholesale Electric sold Erector sets. Figuring a boy could grow into such a toy, Oscar didn't wait until his grandson was old enough to build on his own. Or perhaps he had an extra set left over on Christmas Eve, the last time anyone was likely to buy it for another year. For whatever reason, Larry's grandfather splurged and took home the Sensational No. 7 Erector set.

Plopped on the floor before a five-year-old, the set seemed a gargantuan gift. It came in a red metal box nearly a foot wide and two feet long, with a bright red-and-white label and brass corner trim. Class all the way. When Larry opened the box, random conversation stopped. All attention focused on the toy. Some former boy in the room had probably had an Erector set, but nothing that even approached this one. Like the Lindgren house, Larry's Erector set had an upstairs and a downstairs. Its split levels—a removable tray and the deep bin beneath it—held thirty-two pounds of steel, brass, and boyhood, all ready for assembly with a wrench and a screwdriver, with a paper flag that read "Erector." The set also had a motor, not some battery-powered job but a real plug-in 110-volt motor that Gilbert called the P56G. No sooner was the wrapping torn off than all the men in the family found their way to the floor. Larry was just five, after all. He'd need help. And so the box was opened, the parts unpacked, the building begun. Which of the 399 models in the manual should they build first?

It didn't take long for eight-year-old Elaine to wander over. Standing at the edge of the male pride, she peered over shoulders and bald spots. She wanted to help, too. She had gotten a doll for Christmas, an adorable Patsy to be her "new playmate." She also received a sewing set. Each was okay. Just okay. But there was something about that box and those tiny screws, those red spoked wheels, leaden axles, and brass gears, that spoke to her as surely as did any baseball. Suffering the pure longing known only to children, Elaine made the mistake of asking whether she could play with her cousin's toy. She was quickly chided by the women in the house. "A girl doesn't want an Erector set," she was told. "They're for boys." Elaine looked on, searching for some invitation from a male face. She saw none. Finally she sulked off to a corner and threw herself in a chair. While the men tinkered and the women talked, she put her nose in another volume of the *New Book of Knowledge*—she was plowing through the entire twenty-volume set—and kept it there. Several times she looked over her book to see some strange metal contraption taking shape in front of the tree. She noted the odd effect this toy had on males, making men act like boys, boys like men. Elaine looked, longed, then turned back to her book. It wasn't fair. It just wasn't fair!

When Christmas passed, Elaine visited her cousin every other week. Tromping down narrow stairs to the basement where Larry had the parts spread out on a Ping-Pong table, she asked again and again to play. Every now and then, she got her hands on the set and even built a few things, but not for long. "That was *his* present," she remembered. "And besides, I was a girl and they didn't want to hear any more about it." Several years later, when her younger brother grew to be a real boy, Twentieth Century No. 8 was handed down. To him! Then twelve and slightly more comfortable in dresses, Elaine nonetheless looked "longingly at the intriguing metal parts, picturing how wonderful it would be to make the enticing structures in the Erector set illustrations." But she was still a girl.

A. C. Gilbert did not dislike girls. Nor did he especially like them. If he thought of them at all, it was as pleasant, pretty people who could not be blamed for the regrettable fact that they had not been born boys. That, after all, was their loss. He loved his

two daughters; he maintained a dignified but distancing relationship with the wife he had once called "my dear little girl." But
those girls had each other. He was content with his "boy friends,"
of whom he noted, "I think I may count more of these in the
world than any other single individual." In 1919, Gilbert finally
got a boy friend in his own house, a long-awaited son. But despite his name, Alfred Carleton Gilbert Jr. was still a baby, several
years away from becoming a real "Gilbert boy." And so, moving
into middle age, A. C. Gilbert Sr. lived on his own all-male island.
His childhood memories were as bereft of girls as if he had grown
up in a monastery. He had no sisters. No girls were allowed in his
fire department, nor in the Moscow Athletic Club. The "Dear
Mary" he met in prep school seems to have been his only girlfriend. Yale, like nearly every college in America, was another
pack of men. Once he had graduated and gone into business,
Gilbert's world was peopled exclusively by men, most of them
sporting titles—company presidents, bank vice presidents, chair-
men of the board, directors, officers. . . . His social world re-
volved around men's clubs, every friend a member, director, or
chairman of an athletic club, a yacht club, a chamber of commerce, an alumni group, or the Toy Manufacturers of America.

Such segregation was not unique to Gilbert. He lived in the
age of "separate spheres." Sanctioned by both sexes in books and
magazines throughout the Victorian age and beyond, this sexual
apartheid granted men and women their own domains, separate
but allegedly equal. According to this common wisdom, the male
sphere was the cutthroat world of business, where a man's primal
aggression earned him the bread he took home. The female
sphere was the home, presided over by "the fairer sex," preserv-
ing what decency was left in a world debased by ruthless bread-
winners. The two spheres never intersected, and once courtship
had led to marriage, neither did too many husbands and wives.
They met only for dinner, a Sunday picnic, and occasional conju-
gal visits. Most businessmen sent their families to "the country"
each summer, promising to join them if they could get away from

their work, wink-wink. As the doctrine of separate spheres entered the 1920s, college-educated women chomped at its bit, but
no matter how eloquently they argued for inclusion, the spheres
remained asunder. Sexual segregation didn't need many laws to
make it stick. It reigned in women's societies and ladies' auxiliaries. Its geography was mapped in sewing parlors, at bridge tables, in boxing arenas and baseball bleachers, in lumber and
mining camps, and throughout entire professions where women
needed not apply.

In this context, Gilbert's neglect of girls seems almost benign.
He did not reach out to them, but unlike Elaine Grotefeld's parents, he did not mind if girls, too, made lots of toys. And when allowed access to their brothers' Erector sets, girls didn't mind
either.

In 1915 *Erector Tips* featured a photo of Irene and Virginia
Clare holding two toys they had built with an Erector set, a
merry-go-round and a cradle. Gilbert took the news like a proud
papa. "Two Girls Built These Models!" the magazine headlined
before urging more girls to do the same. "We are glad to notice
that there are girls who are interested in the Erector as well as
boys. We suggest that parents buy for the girls these construction
toys as they give them good ideas regarding mechanical ideas.
Too many women are unacquainted with mechanics, although
they unconsciously apply many mechanical principles to their
home work." The Clare sisters' merry-go-round didn't look like
most boy-built Erector models. A brutish lad might have built a
merry-go-round and left it empty, but the Clare sisters enlivened
theirs with elephants, tigers, and horses ridden by small dolls.
And the cradle, *Erector Tips* posited, "no doubt was designed
after grandma's." In the coming years, girls made other small
encroachments into Gilbert's boy empire. A few feminine names—
such as Lucinda and June—surfaced among the Edgars and
Harolds winning Gilbert's annual contests. One boy and girl
even dared to overlap their spheres. Seven-year-old Ernest South
of Braintree, Massachusetts, shared his Erector set with his sister.

Both entered Gilbert's 1917 contest with a model car they built together. Ernest apparently hadn't heard the latest answers to one of nature's oldest problems.

Gilbert's first Erector set may have solved the boy problem, but once its girders were spread on the floor, the set brought a parallel conundrum home to roost. A girl's brain. A boy's brain. Are they wired the same way? Are girls and boys born blank slates, only to be inscribed by genders so distinct as to be from different planets? If removed from the tyranny of parents, teachers, and peers, would brother and sister prove equally adept at caring for a doll or building a Railroad Signal Tower? In Gilbert's time, academia, society, and common sense scoffed at such a notion. As soon as women enrolled at Smith, Wellesley, and Mount Holyoke Colleges in the 1870s, "scientific" studies began proving—even using statistics!—that women lacked the sterner stuff it took to master the sciences. By the turn of the century, women's college enrollment equaled that of men, yet science remained the most macho house on frat row. The few dozen women with science degrees were refused tenure, given menial lab jobs, and denied membership in scientific societies. The ongoing argument was not pretty. Male professors cited statistics on women's paltry representation in the sciences as proof of female ineptitude in all things empirical. Their female counterparts argued that they were victims of "environment." They were "quite welcome to become experts in washing bottles," one wrote, but were taught from an early age that the only science they could master was that of catching a man. The men told them to stop whining. If they were victims, they were "willing victims." Besides, consider the consequences. A woman might manage a career in some sissy science—psychology or botany, say. But physics? Would you want your mother to handle radium? And what about chemistry? Would you trust your sister to set the periodic table of elements?

Sure, there were exceptions, odd birds like Maria Mitchell. After helping her father chart stars from her backyard on Nantucket Island, Mitchell grew up to discover a comet and teach astronomy at Vassar after the Civil War. But she was the exception that proved the rule. Mitchell and Ellen Richards, first female graduate of MIT (class of 1873), shoved tirelessly against the inertia of popular and academic prejudice. By 1920, prejudice still sat on its throne, puffing a big fat cigar. The everyday chauvinism was best expressed by the *New York Times*. *Some* women might study science, the *Times* editorialized in 1921, but more men "have the power—a necessary qualification for any real achievement in science—of viewing facts abstractly rather than relationally, without overestimating them because they harmonize with previously accepted theories." In short, women were too emotional to be scientists, and the fury they showed when told this only proved the point. Feel free to hiss on cue.

Many mothers, raising daughters in their own image, supported this status quo. So what was to be done with those girls whose shins were perpetually bruised from playing kick-the-can? How was common wisdom to explain away the girls who came home in pinafores filthy from fighting or who looked longingly at an Erector set? For a toy manufacturer, the easiest thing was to ignore them. A few tomboys—even a few thousand across the nation—did not mean that Gilbert's "practical boy psychology" had to don a dress. His institute remained the Gilbert Institute of Engineering for Boys. His clubs remained Gilbert Boys' Clubs. And he never broadened his slogan beyond "Hello, Boys!" nor did anyone take him to task for it. Face it, girls. This was America. In France, Marie Curie had won Nobel Prizes in chemistry and physics. Curie toured America in 1921 to great fanfare, accepting honorary degrees from twenty universities, speaking in Carnegie Hall, meeting President Harding at the White House. But the women scientists who escorted her, even those with doctorates, were eking out careers as lab assistants and professors at women's colleges. Meanwhile, other women with a passion for lab work toiled in the only science they could call their own—home economics.

After fifty years as an academic movement, home economics came into the home in 1920. Shelves of books promoted "household engineering," often as a correspondence course. Reading industrial-strength prose touting "standardized conditions" and "scientific management," women learned to make their homes models of efficiency. Housewives mastered the chemistry of cooking and mapped out efficient kitchens with the sink near dish cabinets, the oven near the serving table, and so on. "Is not housework as worthwhile studying as the shoveling of coal?" asked Mrs. Christine Frederick, Household Efficiency Engineer. "Is not housekeeping the biggest, the most essential industry of all?" Yet even following Frederick's ideal schedule, the average "household engineer" put in six thirteen-hour days of washing, cooking, and cleaning.

With such a career ahead of her, only a mother a half century ahead of her time would have suggested that Elaine Grotefeld play with an Erector set. If the playroom was a garden of budding adults, a boy needed wrenches and screwdrivers. All a girl needed was a doll. And as the toy business mushroomed after World War I, dolls proliferated like babies themselves. A generation before, most dolls were made from rags, corn husks, or clothespins, but the girl of the 1920s was primed for the full Barbie treatment. For the first time, soft plastic heads, flexible limbs, and brushable hair made a doll a miniature of its owner. Girls had always cared for dolls as their own children. Now dolls became friends with distinct personalities and cuddly names like Soozie Smiles. Like Barbie, many of these dolls came with complete lines of accessories. When a girl tired of mothering, she could do other "woman's work" writ small, cooking in her toy kitchen, doing laundry in her toy washing machine, rearranging her doll's house with the precision of a household engineer.

A girl's playroom was her sorority, its manners and morals strictly enforced. Yet beyond this sanctuary, a girl's role models were changing in ways that even Gilbert couldn't help but notice. A quarter of all married women now worked outside the home, many of them in Gilbert's factory. Single women were stepping out. Some even smoked in public! Others were trying on morals and makeup that mocked Victorian values. These days, such trends would trickle down into toys, spawning a Flapper Barbie or "23 Skidoo Career Game." Yet toys of the 1920s, manufactured mostly by men, remained rooted in unrefined sexism. Ignoring all evidence of a "new woman," girl toys remained as demure as men like Louis Marx and A. C. Gilbert wanted their daughters to be. So when Gilbert finally released his first full line of toys for girls, he named it after the most demure woman he knew, his sister-in-law with the elegant name.

LaVelle Young, like Mary Gilbert a prim lady from the Pacific Northwest, had married Frank Wellington Gilbert. Frank, eight years younger than A. C., had followed his older brother to Yale and, after graduating in 1916, joined the A. C. Gilbert Company as a general foreman. He was bright, eager, and "wide-awake," a gentle man with a gift for getting along. More congenial than his exacting brother, Frank was also skilled at designing the machines that designed toys. Sharing A. C.'s preference for initials, Frank was known around the New Haven plant as F. W. What F. W.'s wife, LaVelle, knew about toys could be confined to the playthings belonging to her two young children. Yet in 1922 Gilbert (A. C., not F. W.) used LaVelle as the symbol fronting his LaVelle Toys, "made especially for girls." That February, while a mah-jongg craze began to captivate the nation, the LaVelle line debuted at the New York Toy Fair. In eighth-floor rooms in the Hotel Breslin, toy buyers saw LaVelle's Little Dressmaker, Pla-Klay, sewing sets, a Little Cook chef's set, the World War I Nurse's Outfit, and a Little Laundress set. LaVelle also included some of the earliest kiddie phonograph records. Her only hint that some girls might be tomboyish came when the LaVelle line, for reasons hard to fathom, included a Yale-Harvard Football Game and a Tip-Top Boxing Game.

LaVelle Gilbert may have been as nurturing as the photo that showed her, short-haired and very post-Victorian, on each ad.

But LaVelle toys were nothing special, and girls knew it. Not all girls wanted Erector sets, but neither did they clamor for Pla-Klay, a precursor to Play-Doh. Or perhaps they couldn't figure out how to correctly misspell the name. Two years after LaVelle Toys hit the market, they were discounted by 33 percent. Throughout the Depression, the toys struggled on, getting no attention from Gilbert himself. They finally disappeared from Gilbert's line, replaced by more toys for boys.

Meanwhile, the girl problem outlasted the 1920s. During the Depression, despite the advancements of women, girls were expected to be more like Shirley Temple than Amelia Earhart. Their toys excluded any play that demanded reason, construction, or knowing your way around a toolbox. Unsolved when Elaine Grotefeld clamored to play with her cousin's Erector set, the problem found at least one answer during World War II, when Rosie the Riveter posters told girls "We can do it!" The solution came not from toys or society at large but from progressive parents.

When Marian Kaplun turned five, her parents bought an Erector set. She had no brothers or sisters. The set was for her. Other parents on her block in the Bronx were shocked. "They didn't want a girl to play with boy toys, but I didn't like doll carriages," she remembered. "I always climbed highest in the playground, skated backward, and did all the things boys did but girls weren't allowed to do." David Kaplun, a welfare administrator, and his wife, Bertha, a social worker, saw nothing wrong with their daughter building things with real structural steel. David was teaching Marian the violin, so why not let her develop dexterity with nuts and bolts? For the next two years, the Kapluns' living room was a construction site, littered with steel sleds, seesaws, and wheelbarrows. By the time Marian turned seven, she was ready to upgrade. As Christmas approached in 1946, her father asked her to choose a gift that met the family's $5 limit. He suggested crayons, coloring books, tops, or those bouncy pink rubber balls known in the Bronx and Brooklyn as "spaldeens."

Then David noted that $5 would also buy a motor for his daughter's Erector set. "I thought and thought and thought about it," Marian recalled. "Finally, it was clear to me I wanted the motor."

Motors house magnets to spin their shafts, but Marian's had a second kind of magnetism. "It was a real boy magnet," she remembered. "Boys from all over the neighborhood kept dropping in to play." Working in her living room, Marian and her boy friends built motorized carousels, trucks, and drawbridges. They made a Ferris wheel and shared it with Marian's third-grade class during show-and-tell. Sometimes some local Jimmy or Biff, awash in the ambient machismo, suggested that boys could build better than girls, nyaaah, nyaaah! Marian didn't care. She was a walking lesson in gender equality rare for the Bronx in the 1940s. "All the boys told me Erector sets weren't for girls, but it didn't bother me. My parents were very enlightened, and I was brought up to be whatever I wanted to be." When not toying with her Erector set, Marian became Little Ms. Fix-it around the apartment. She fixed her father's music stand, even repaired broken clocks. "We couldn't afford to replace broken things, so it was fix it or don't have it anymore."

Marian played with her Erector set until she entered junior high. There she and all other suspected tomboys were set straight by the toughest gender cops of all—other girls. "Suddenly I wanted to be like everyone else if I could possibly manage it. I wouldn't have dreamed of not being like other girls. I became tremendously conventional." Instead of a screwdriver, Marian became very handy with lipstick. She abandoned her Erector set. Like so many others, it disappeared from her memory. She has no idea where it went to rust, yet she remembers its lessons. She did not grow up to be an engineer, preferring instead to teach English, but when she later became a psychologist, she recalled the therapeutic value of tinkering. A corner of her office in Massachusetts now includes several construction toys—Legos, blocks, and a modern Erector set. Construction toys are still good for what ails you, she says, if what ails you is an urge to make something out of your life. Dr. Marian Kaplun Shapiro helps patients overcome anxiety and depression by letting them build, and by sharing her own stories of building as a metaphor for constructing personality and success.

By the time Marian Kaplun had forsaken her Erector set, Gilbert was softening in his old age. He did not give up on traditional girl toys, continuing to sell a whole line of girl-size furniture after World War II. But girls, once relegated to LaVelle's side of the family, began to appear in Erector ads during the 1950s. "What will they be doing in 1970?" an ad asked beneath a boy and a girl playing with Gilbert's toys. Still, vestiges of the problem lingered. In the ad, the boy is tightening the screws on a towering Erector radar dish. His sister is merely weighing chemicals on a toy scale. In 1970, the ad suggested, he'd be the lead engineer, she some lowly assistant. Girls were still girls, and if they were to be enticed by a microscope, it had to come in a pink box, as Gilbert's first microscope for girls did in 1958. Color and gender, however, did not concern Wendy Christensen, who got her Erector set that year for her sixth birthday.

In an old family snapshot, an unmistakable joy fills Wendy's face as she opens her Erector set. "I was always a gadget fiend," Christensen remembers. "I was born that way. I always liked to tinker." Wendy's father, an electrical engineer in southern California's booming aerospace industry of the 1950s, designed equipment for submarines. Her mother just kept washing, cleaning, and caring for kids, ten in all. There must have been other engineer's daughters on the block, but only Donald Christensen encouraged his little girl's machine dreams. "My father used to take me down to the Burbank airport to watch the planes. I wanted to grow up to be a test pilot. I wanted to fly the X-15." Once she opened her Erector set, Wendy developed a fascination with its minute precision. "I loved the little tiny screws," she said. "I still love little tiny parts, pieces of jewelry, and any attention to detail." Boys on the block, still slaves to stereotyping, told her

Erector sets weren't for girls. Wendy told them to take their Davy Crockett caps and take a hike. "I was one of those kids who didn't fit into any group," she remembered. "I was always an oddball. I still am an oddball. I got used to being one at an early age."

When she was eighteen, Wendy applied to study computer programming at a technical training school, one of those "institutes" that advertised on late-night TV. Although feminism was then in full flower, she was told the subject was too hard for women. Denied admission, she studied programming at UCLA night school, then became a software engineer for the aerospace company where her father worked. After several years, she moved to the New Hampshire woods to pursue her other loves—art and cats. Her illustrations, as minutely detailed as any Erector schematic, now appear in cat calendars and magazines. She also does technical writing on the side. "My Erector set was an important part of my development," she said. "What was really special about those toys was the wondrous precision of the pieces. There was something about them that left an impression on me."

The girl problem has yet to be solved, but cracks have appeared in the castle walls that once kept the scientific kingdom safe from females at the gates. Since 1970, advanced degrees in physical sciences for women have risen from about 6 percent to nearly 25 percent of the nation's total. The gains are even more dramatic in bachelor's degrees. Yet resistance now takes subtler forms. Women scientists are more likely than their male counterparts to be underemployed in industry and off tenure track in academia. And there is something about the nuts and bolts of engineering that still seems, well, a guy thing. Women now earn more than a third of all bachelor's degrees in the physical sciences and more than half of all such degrees in the biological sciences. In engineering, however, they take home just one of every six bachelor of science degrees. So the question remains: A boy's brain. A girl's brain.

Generalizations about gender are like quicksand. Many an expert has tried to guide others safely through them, only to end up with a lot of explaining to do. In contrast to Gilbert's time, few would now dare suggest that engineering is beyond a woman's ability. Yet some psychologists cautiously hint at certain tendencies. Just as girls (in general) run circles around boys (in general) in reading, boys (in general) are better 3-D thinkers. Shown an object on paper, they can more easily describe how it would look from behind, above, or to the side, a critical skill in the making of a person who designs machines. Of course, nothing will ever prove that the skill is inborn. It may be a matter of right brain vs. left brain, the former dominating spatial thinking; the latter, linguistics. Boys tend to be more right-brained; girls, left-brained. Or it may be a question of who has "the right brain," i.e., the type of brain society and schools reward for its innate abilities. Harvard psychologist Howard Gardner theorizes that males evolved superior spatial abilities because envisioning a landscape was vital for hunting and gathering. Whichever theory you embrace, these days the girl problem can still be blamed on toys, which remain stubbornly divided by gender. The geared and motorized toys are still marketed to boys; the cuter and cuddlier are found on the pastel aisle in the toy store. And aside from a few astronauts, where are the visible role models—the female mechanical engineers, electrical engineers, and everyday mechanics—necessary to inspire any girl to storm the walls of science? The problem remains; the argument continues, and it still isn't pretty.

Yet even if boys may be from MIT and girls from Wellesley, women who solved the girl problem learned more from their Erector sets than how to get an engineering degree. They learned that building can be as much an art as a science. "Even now I look at a suspension bridge and marvel at it," said Sidhartha Gabriel Ellis, whose father gave her an Erector set and other "boy toys" after he and his wife lost their first two sons, one boy stillborn,

*O*n the track at Yale University, Gilbert won national championships and set world records in the pole vault.

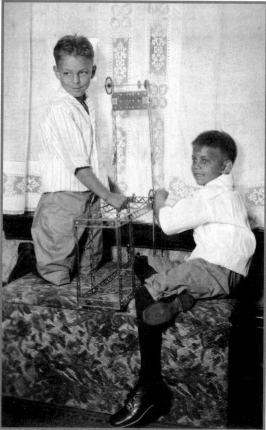

*T*wo budding geniuses prepare for the future with their early (pre-1924) Erector set.

*T*his 1915 Erector ad suggested A. C. Gilbert's view of a boy's split personality.

*I*n 1915 the top prize in Gilbert's Erector design contest was a real automobile, a Trumbull, valued at $395.

Games, puzzles, and kits for every conceivable science came from the Gilbert factory in its heyday.

RICHARD WALKER

In the early 1920s, the Gilbert Circus Car brought Erector and other toys to kids in small towns from Massachusetts to the Midwest.

GILBERT FAMILY COLLECTION

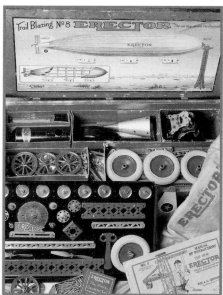

Half the fun of an Erector set was just opening the box and gazing at all the parts. This Trailblazing No. 8 built a zeppelin five feet long.

RICHARD WALKER

*G*ilbert acquired American Flyer trains in 1937. His improvements, including engines that smoked and whistled, made them serious rivals to Lionel.

GILBERT FAMILY COLLECTION

*A*merica's oldest boy hobnobs with other "Gilbert boys" at the opening of the Gilbert Hall of Science in Manhattan in 1941.

RAY MORHLANG

*A*lways seeking new models, Gilbert introduced this carousel in the 1949 No. 10½ Amusement Park Erector set.

RICHARD WALKER

*I*n 1950 the Gilbert Atomic Energy kit let Brylcreemed boys play with radioactive cloud chambers and other tools of the nuclear age.

*U*ndeterred by sexist stereotypes about girls, Wendy Christensen knew just what she wanted for her sixth birthday. Here she opens her very own Erector set back in 1958.

*I*t wasn't easy being A. C. Gilbert Jr., but Al Gilbert did his best, eventually becoming president of his father's company.

*G*ilbert's widely used publicity photograph showed a dour executive and his creation.

GILBERT FAMILY COLLECTION

*T*he King of Connecticut takes a rare moment to relax beside his hunting lodge in Paradise.

GILBERT FAMILY COLLECTION

*E*rector collector Bill Klein tinkers with a model at the A. C. Gilbert Heritage Society's 2001 convention in Carlisle, Pennsylvania.

*M*echanical engineer Mark Summers used his Erector set to help design Soarin' Over California, one of the most popular attractions at Disney's California Adventure park in Anaheim.

*T*he world's largest Erector design is in the backyard of A. C. Gilbert's Discovery Village in Salem, Oregon. The children's museum features a room of Erector sets and other Gilbert memorabilia.

*T*here are hundreds of Erector set collectors, but most agree that the best collection belongs to Bill Bean of Dayton, Ohio.

RICHARD WALKER

*J*hough he retired in 1954, Gilbert tried to stay active in advertising his company. Above, he displays the creations of the mid-1950s Erector sets, including the famous Walking Robot

*J*oward the end of his life, Gilbert shows off a newspaper column about his career.

another miscarried. "My father made a big thing out of demonstrating basic principles with my Erector set. One time I put the wheels on a car too tight, and it wouldn't go. He explained you have to leave them a little loose. It sounds simple, but to a child, it opens a whole world. Now I understand how things are put together. When you're little, everything looks so big and so grown-up. Erector sets brought the world down to size."

Sandra's seen a leprechaun,
Eddie touched a troll,
Laurie danced with witches once,
Charlie found some goblins' gold.
Donald heard a mermaid sing,
Suzy spied an elf,
But all the magic I have known
I've had to make myself.
—SHEL SILVERSTEIN

7

Natural Wonders

Dit-daa-dit-dit . . . December 24, 1906—As the sun sets over the Atlantic seaboard, dozens of merchant ships are cruising off the coast of New England. The weather is better than anyone has a right to expect on Christmas Eve. Light clouds and fog, no snow expected, temperatures in the teens. That night, a fourteen-year-old boy wandering alone in the marshes of Westchester County will freeze to death in his knickers. He will be found on Christmas morning, a mystery, a corpse with stiff, twisted limbs huddled beside muddy footprints showing where the boy stumbled, sought refuge, stumbled again, and fell. Yet sailors at sea are safe and almost warm. Bound for port or the open ocean, they are spending a lonely, quiet holiday. On each ship, the scene is similar. As darkness descends, cooks serve makeshift Christmas dinners while seamen drink, sing, or just suffer a long, silent night. In radio rooms, each ship's wireless operator taps out Morse code and listens to staccato replies. *Dit-dit-daa-daa-dit-dit.* Static occasionally washes over a signal. A whine or a whistle interferes. Then again—*dit-daa-dit-dit-daa-dit.*

At a precise time lost to history, something supernatural comes across the face of the waters. From out of the white noise and fog, dots and dashes spell out CQ, CQ—Morse code for "stand by for communication." Then in headphones all up and down the coast, wireless operators pick up a miracle beamed through "the ether." Faintly, very faintly, they hear the sound of a human voice. A man speaking!

Within minutes, radio rooms are crowded with disbelievers. No one has ever heard a voice over a wireless, and many aren't sure they're hearing it now. Headphones are passed from operator to captain, from captain to first mate, and on down the chain of command. Each man hears the voice. Then after a few moments, each hears things equally astonishing. A woman singing. A violin playing "O Holy Night." A man reading from the Book of Luke. Through the headphones, the tinny voice fades in and out while reciting familiar words: "And there were in the same country shepherds out in the field, keeping watch over their flocks by night. And an angel of the Lord appeared to them, and the glory of the Lord shone around them." Perhaps some men get down on their knees. Some may run from the room. Others simply listen. When the biblical verses conclude, a man thanks his audience. He asks listeners to please send him a card care of R. A. Fessenden, Brant Rock, Massachusetts, telling him where they picked up his signal. And he announces he will have another broadcast on New Year's Eve. Then he signs off. The airwaves surrender to the staccato. Waves lap against bows. Fogs roll in and out. But the ether and its inhabitants will never again be so quiet or so lonely.

Some have said that if there is magic on this planet, it is in water. But by the dawn of the twentieth century, water's secrets were well known. From Niagara to the open sea, people had seen all water had to show them. Water was always drowning some loved one, flooding a hometown, drenching a picnic or parade. Luckily, the natural world had other wizards ready to step into the lime-light. The magician of the moment was galena. A leaden gray crystal often found in perfect cubes, galena had the remarkable ability to detect Hertzian waves, later known as radio waves. These bursts of electromagnetic energy were created by a spark jumping a gap between two electrodes. First at a distance of a few miles, later amped up to travel between cities, radio waves were gathered by galena or sometimes by silicon, iron pyrite, or another of nature's pure crystals. Throughout the 1890s and early 1900s, the secrets of "wireless telegraphy" spread through the scientific community. By the time Gilbert was at Yale, hundreds of hobbyists were toying with crystal sets. A simple crystal on a table, touched by a filament nicknamed a "cat's whisker," then wired to a coil of copper and a pair of headphones, could pick up dots, dashes, and eventually human voices from out of nowhere. You didn't even need one of Edison's batteries. Voices coming through rocks. If this wasn't magic, what was?

Much of the early tinkering was done by boys. These pioneers of the airwaves sequestered themselves in garages, clamping big black discs around their ears. Members of school "wireless clubs" wound wire tuners around any available cylinders—baseball bats, toilet paper tubes, Quaker Oats boxes. Grounding one wire on a faucet or fence post, they touched another to the tallest metal they could find. Leaning closer, they slid a piece of metal along the tuner coil and threw their hopes beyond the nearest hill. On the far side of that hill, makeshift 100-watt transmitters beamed signals from radio stations set up in department stores, universities, banks, newspaper offices. A boy never knew what might come through his crystal set in those days. Sopranos were common. A fat lady singing signaled the start, not the end, of a program. Slide the metal along the coil. Pause. "Shhhhh. I'm getting something." In mid-sentence, a weather report came from . . . where? Maine? Maryland? Naah, just New Jersey. Slide the metal again. *Dit-daa-dit-dit.* Tickle the cat's whisker. The sudden *caaaaaaaahh* of static . . . *Hisssssssss* . . . Then someone playing a saxophone. Jiggle the antenna wire. *Caaaaaaaaahh! Whiiiiii-innnnnne! Wheeeeoooooo!* A voice! "—rico Caruso live from the Metropolitan Opera in New York!" Hey, I'm picking up Caruso! No, I'm serious. C'mere! Listen!

The miracle of voices from rocks could not remain amateur for long. Commercial interests are a force of human nature, and shortly after World War I, they began gathering momentum. On election night in 1920, the nation's first licensed radio station, KDKA in Pittsburgh, broadcast returns tallying a clear victory for Warren Harding. Other stations soon followed. WBZ in Springfield, Massachusetts. WDY in Roselle Park, New Jersey. KYW in Chicago. Then in September 1921, the nation's fifth licensed station, WCJ, went on the air, broadcasting from the A. C. Gilbert factory.

Atop the rear of his plant fronting the New York, New Haven & Hartford Railroad tracks, Gilbert erected a 125-foot transmitting tower. Tall and slender atop the squat brick building, the tower looked as if it had been built from some mammoth Erector set. Before his transmitter could handle voice, Gilbert broadcast in Morse code. Throughout New England, boys in barns and woodsheds listened in on jury-rigged wireless sets or on their own Gilbert Wireless Outfit, a beginner's set with a "Radiotector," aka crystal, selling for $25. Jotting down dots and dashes, boys translated them into words: "We have established a high-powered radio transmitter in our plant here in New Haven under special government license, and will send daily press messages and matters of general interest. The operator in charge of the Gilbert station will transmit the daily news twice every day except Saturday and Sunday. . . . Each of the periods will be used to transmit at different speeds. This will give the beginner, as well as the experienced operator, an opportunity to copy the press bulletins."

Soon boys began hearing voices in their headphones straight from WCJ. The news came in loud and clear, but who was that singing? Gilbert, in an effort to fill air time, had gone downstairs to gather impromptu quartets made up of his employees. A quartet was followed by a guest speaker from Yale, then more news: "Another strike has hit the garment industry. The nation now has sixty-nine labor strikes under way, an all-time high. Britain and France have urged America to join the League of Nations. Russian refugees are fleeing famine-stricken Samara. And in the third inning of today's game at the Polo Grounds in New York, Babe Ruth broke his own home-run record, hitting his fifty-ninth round-tripper!" Then WCJ signed off, leaving boys to ponder the magic.

Towering over the tracks, emblazoned with huge letters spelling out ERECTOR, Gilbert's transmitter remained a New Haven landmark for the next half century. The daily broadcasts, however, were short-lived. For a few years, Gilbert manufactured elaborate radio equipment—amplifiers, speakers, headphones. Then in 1923, sued by RCA over the use of certain tubes, he gave up the entire line. "I have always tried to ride in too many directions at once as it is," he noted years later when the medium he had abandoned dwarfed the toy business. "Radio was not just another bypath, but a main road. And I already had one laid out for me."

It was another A. C., science fiction writer Arthur C. Clarke, who noted the link between science and illusion. "Any sufficiently advanced technology is indistinguishable from magic," Clarke observed. And in the 1920s, just about any technology seemed sufficiently advanced to qualify. Science was putting a "Presto!" into ordinary lives. During the decade, radio brought the excitement of ballrooms and ballparks into living rooms. Refrigeration created the modern kitchen. Automobiles became the transport of the common man. Electricity, which wired just a third of all American homes in 1920, lit up two-thirds by 1930. And as science became the wizard of Main Street, Gilbert brought its marvels down to size. He had already sold millions of engineering kits called Erector sets. Now he would try to do the same for science, explaining its mysteries in a way any boy could understand.

Schools could teach scientific formulas, but Gilbert knew that a boy was only challenged by things that jumped the gap and sent a spark through his brain. Flashes of light! Voices from the ether! Explosions—well, maybe just a minor ka-boom. In short, a boy gravitated toward anything that defied the daily drudgery of a town where you were here today and here tomorrow, where adults had all the power and nothing was ever going to change except you'd get older and get married and have kids who'd be as bored as you were. Could science, Mr. Gilbert, offer something more than that?

The playroom of the 1920s was no house of the intellect. If toys had IQs—the new icon of intelligence was a fad of the decade—most would have tested on the uphill slope of the bell curve. Popular toys of the decade included big brawny steel trucks called "Buddy L" (estimated IQ 67); dolls from popular comic strips such as *Krazy Kat, Barney Google,* and *Felix the Cat* (IQ 73); and "Hey Hey the Chicken Snatcher," which, when wound up, made a dog chomp the rear end of a black chicken thief (IQ 58). The decade's best-selling toy was an old Chinese trick repackaged and sold by Louis Marx—the yo-yo (IQ too low to measure). But while these toys were searching for a lowest common denominator, one toy company dared to treat boys as if they were budding geniuses.

In 1920 Gilbert put out kits in fourteen separate sciences and skills. Their manuals were written by scientists from Yale, Columbia, and General Electric. The toy trade had never seen such an intelligent line of toys before, and nothing like it has been seen since: Gilbert Light Experiments. Gilbert Sound Experiments. Gilbert Civil Engineering. Gilbert Hydraulic and Pneumatic Engineering. Gilbert Mineralogy. Gilbert Magnetic Fun and Facts. Gilbert Weather Bureau. Gilbert Electrical Set. Gilbert Tele-set. Gilbert Signal Engineering, with "a big book on signals written by a man who was formerly in the Signal Division of the U.S. Navy." Gilbert Glass Blowing. Gilbert Soldering Outfit. Gilbert Wireless Outfit.

Gilbert Carpentry. Supplementing the kits was Gilbert's Master Hand Library, 80-page books on each of the above plus *Gilbert Knots and Splices, Gilbert Coin Tricks,* and *Gilbert Handkerchief Tricks.* And along with *Erector Tips,* Gilbert began publishing a yearbook featuring articles with titles like "Noted Civil Engineers and Their Work" and "Prominent Figures in the World of Sports," and his own tips on pole vaulting. So there it is, boys. What do you want to be when you grow up? Why not start today?

The professors who wrote Gilbert's manuals might have been satisfied to train future scientists, but he knew boys wanted more out of life than lab work. In his stump speeches before business groups, he often spoke for the all-American boy. "Ask a boy who he would like to be," he said, "and every boy would name a leader. Ask him who he would rather not be and he would quickly answer—'a quitter, coward, cheat, or a fellow who did not know how to play the game.'" To attract future leaders, Gilbert marketed his kits with a time-tested allure. Three centuries earlier, the philosopher Francis Bacon had written, "Knowledge is power, not mere argument or ornament." Now America's leading toy maker was bringing Bacon's wisdom to the playground. In magazine ads, Gilbert equated science with power and popularity: "The boy who knows about different kinds of engineering—electrical, chemical, structural, etc.—the kinds that are covered by Gilbert Toys, is the type of boy who will be a leader among his fellow boy friends. He is the boy whom the rest of the boys look up to, and they only do it because they appreciate that he has a knowledge of different things which they don't understand."

But what kinds of knowledge? Was the average boy dying to learn surveying right in his own backyard? Could he be trusted with a soldering iron? A saw? A glassblowing kit? Gilbert thought he could be, especially when trying to amaze his friends.

A few of Gilbert's kits were mere textbooks with tools. There was not much legerdemain to be found in civil engineering, telegraphy, or sending signals by semaphore. But whenever science could be sold as supernatural, the magician surfaced in Gilbert's manuals. Gilbert Light Experiments taught boys the basics—light is made of all colors; it travels at 186,000 miles per second. The kit helped boys play with shadows and make a periscope, a camera obscura, and a simple photometer. More advanced sections explained how movies work and how the eye is constructed. Then, with the heavy lifting done, it was time for "illusions."

ILLUSIONS: THE SPHINX.

This illusion shows an Egyptian head without a body. The hypnotist shows the audience an empty box with a glass front. He closes and locks the door over the front, places the box exactly on the center of the table, unlocks it, opens the door, and behold, there is an Egyptian head in the box.

The optical magician speaks: "O ancient Sphinx, awake!" The head slowly opens its eyes. The audience gasps! The eyes blink, sending shivers through the crowd. The magician then asks the Sphinx questions, which it answers "in very deep and very dead tones." Magic? When seen from the back row, perhaps, but it was all done with two large mirrors hiding the Sphinx's body, crouching beneath the table. The same setup made a Pharaoh's Thumb, "dried but not decomposed," appear. With prompting, the thumb answered the pressing questions of the neighborhood. A forward dip of the digit meant yes! Earl would get that bicycle he wanted. A still thumb signaled no. Jimmy's little sister would not be sold to gypsies. Gilbert Sound Experiments offered a similar blend of science and hocus-pocus, its experiments ranging from tin-can telephones to "how to make a lead weight ding" by using "thought waves."

The most unusual of all Gilbert's kits made hydraulic engineers out of boys whose mothers were convinced they'd catch pneumonia if they got the least bit wet. Anyone could show a boy a good time with magnets, but it took Gilbert to turn plumbing into backyard fun. The Gilbert Hydraulic and Pneumatic Engineering kit was a future plumber's Erector set. It contained a tin tank, a bottle, an assortment of glass and rubber tubes, stoppers, and spigots, and every plumber's best friend—a toy submarine. Following the instructions, boys rigged up small city water systems. Setting spigots at different heights, they compared water pressure in upstairs and downstairs faucets. Then, the manual taught boys how to use hydraulics to win a "BIG GUN BATTLE." Mighty jets of water sank tin cans and cups in bathtubs. Rapid-fire water guns attacked "forts, trenches, tanks, etc." Archimedes, eat your heart out! Finally, if some spoilsport parent didn't rush in with towels and promises of "a licking you'll never forget," the boy could learn some serious science: to calculate the pressure on a depth bomb, simply multiply surface area by depth by the density of water and divide by 144. Be sure to write your answer in pounds per square inch. Altogether, the kit featured 129 pages of hydraulic and pneumatic high jinks. Whether boys became engineers, plumbers, or just the best squirt gun marksmen on their block, they learned to appreciate things they had taken for granted, things like air and water. After all, "most boys take things too much for granted," Gilbert wrote. "It is the clever boy who digs into things and finds out the reasons."

Blending science with magic, Gilbert jump-started the educational toy business. Any kid who has ever owned a chemistry set, microscope, or other scaled-down scientific instrument can thank Gilbert. And as he became a household name, Gilbert earned plenty of gratitude. Gilbert's fan mail now averaged 2,000 letters a day, many from lads too young to capitalize the first-person pronoun. Gilbert fondly called these his "little 'i' letters." "Dear Mr. Giblet," one boy wrote, "i wonder could you give me a idea where i can get a book on forward passing and receiving. i am not very good on the receiving. i can't keep aholt of it." Many such letters were signed, "Your loving son." Parents, too, wrote to the man who seemed to know their sons so well. "Dear Mr. Gilbert," began a handwritten note dated December 1923, "I do not know how much money you have made this year, but I do know that you have brought happiness to hundreds of thousands of American boys. I am certain that your Xmas will be filled with Joy, for you have given to many a lad his first glimpse into a Future that is bright with opportunity. May the best things of life be yours." The sender could rest assured that Gilbert was making plenty of money. The company had a new plant in Austria, along with sales offices in several American cities and in Toronto, London, and Paris. Gilbert was taking home $50,000 a year, equivalent to more than $500,000 these days. Such unbridled success made it seem an unlikely time to revamp the company's main product, yet Gilbert was planning radical changes in Erector. Soon the biggest sets would nearly give Dad a hernia bringing one home. But while plotting these changes, Gilbert came up with "probably the best promotion and advertising idea I ever had." The idea harked back to his boyhood, when traveling magicians came through Moscow, Idaho. This time, however, the traveling show would conjure up the mysteries of science and the simple joy of building things.

Throughout the rolling green farmland of eastern Pennsylvania, the excitement arrived a few days before the train. After rolling down through the Appalachians, word reached Reading in the June 27, 1922, edition of the *Reading Eagle*.

IT'S HEADED OUR WAY!

WILL ARRIVE JUNE 29, 1922

GET YOUR TICKET NOW

for the wonderful Private Car exhibition of all the famous Gilbert Toys—see the fascinating array of operating models never before shown—hear concerts on the marvelous wireless telephone. It's all free. Brought to this city at tremendous cost. The only thing of its kind. Never before have you been given such an opportunity. Don't miss it.

Once word was out, it spread along a wireless network that ran through backyards and front porches, alleys and ball fields.

"Mr. Gilbert's coming to town. Well, maybe not him. But maybe him! His train, anyway."

"What are you yappin' about?"

"A train car. A big old train car. Filled with Erector sets!

And chemistry sets! And wireless and all that other neat stuff. And maybe Mr. Gilbert himself, who knows? It's coming to Reading. On Thursday."

"Who's Mr. Gilbert?"

"You don't know who—?"

"'Course she don't. She's a girl."

"Mr. Gilbert's the man—"

"Save your breath. She's a girl. So how do we see him? We need tickets?"

"You get 'em at Neubling's."

"Cost anything?"

"Nope. Free."

"Lez go 'a Neubling's then."

While the news spread, the Gilbert train car wound its way along the tracks. On June 22 and 23, it was in Scranton, where it was met by a scruffy crew of boys and men, many of them hungrier and angrier than usual owing to a nationwide anthracite coal strike that was entering its thirteenth week. The following day, a Saturday, it reached Wilkes-Barre, just downriver from Pittston, where Harold Heal was driving his own convertible and too busy for kids' stuff. After observing the Sabbath, the train rolled into Hazelton on Monday, then went south to Shenandoah on Tuesday and Pottstown the following day. Finally, it rumbled into a town where nuts and bolts were the stuff of daily life.

A hardscrabble city of industries, Reading earned its living by the sweat of its citizens. Beneath the shadow of Neversink Mountain, Reading's families, most of them German immigrants, worked long days in furnaces, foundries, machine shops, textile mills, and tobacco processing plants. Most of America had begun sending its adolescents to high school, but in Reading, half the population between sixteen and eighteen years old was fully employed. So on Thursday morning, although Neubling's and five other stores had given out hundreds of tickets, hardly any kids— boys or girls—were on hand when a steam locomotive pulling a long train car hissed to a stop at the Reading station.

The train car was shaped like a regular Pullman, yet it had been done up as if P. T. Barnum, playing Monopoly, had paid his $200 for the Reading Railroad and turned it into a circus train. From end to end the car was bright yellow, topped by a gaudy green roof. On each end, ten-foot-tall ads flanked the car's long, flat middle. One ad showed a boy in white shirt and tie holding a catalog of Gilbert Toys. The other featured a polar bear standing before a Polar Cub fan. In between, four-foot red letters spelled out "GILBERT TOYS." Smaller lettering announced: "RADIO TELEPHONE—MUSIC, VOICES THROUGH THE AIR"; "SCIENTIFIC TOYS—EDUCATIONAL FUNMAKERS"; and "ERECTOR—WORLD FAMOUS CONSTRUCTION TOY."

As it was shunted onto a siding in the yard at the foot of Penn Street, three men got out and began fanning themselves in the shade. They glanced around as if to ask, What podunk town are we in today? Moments later, they went back inside to begin preparing the car. During the late morning, a few boys knocked on the rear door and asked to see inside. They were told to come back at three-thirty that afternoon. That's when the show would start. Then the men continued their work. They took science kits and Erector sets out of cabinets and set them up "in all their glory," as Mr. Gilbert had instructed. They raised a twenty-five-foot antenna above the car and strung it with flapping flags, then hoisted the Stars and Stripes from the pole at the far end. Their work done, the men sauntered along Penn Street toward downtown to see if there might be a decent diner in Reading, maybe even a speakeasy where a guy could get a beer. In midafternoon, they came back to the railroad yard to find more than a hundred heads surrounding the train car.

Boys wrestled on the periphery of the crowd. Closer to the car, hands pointed out ads. Some boys swore they saw Mr. Gilbert's face in the window. Small bets were taken on the matter. Hearts were crossed with hopes to die. Whole stacks of hypothetical Bibles were sworn upon. And then, as the hour drew near, more kids arrived. Above the steeples and factory towers, the sky threatened rain. A few parents stood languidly to the side holding umbrellas in one hand, small, sweaty palms in the other. When would it start? Finally, a man in a dark suit stepped onto the platform and asked the kids to please form a line alongside the car. After much pushing and shoving, the line extended from the yard down the street to the nearest foundry, its hellish red fire visible through open doors. Finally, at exactly 3:30 P.M., the rear door opened. In groups of two and three, kids filed up the narrow steps and into the train car that had brought the A. C. Gilbert Company to the Reading line.

Inside, the car was cool and cramped. At the front of a long narrow aisle stood a magician in top hat and tails. Fanning a deck of cards, he asked one wide-eyed boy to "pick a card, any card." Moving past him, kids met the man they had seen on the platform. He flipped a switch, and an Erector elevator rose in its shaft. As all eyes followed it, the elevator descended, then rose again. Boys pointed to glass cases holding Erector models they had built or wished they could. Owners of buck-a-box sets ogled the giant three-layer wooden cases. If they could just get their hands on one of those. Thirty bucks? How long would it take to save that much? Let's see, with a nickel allowance . . . As one boy calculated, others walked deeper into the car to see the whole line of Gilbert kits—from Gilbert Carpentry to the Gilbert Weather Bureau. Each lid was open, each kit promising to make a leader out of the rank and file.

"Look, there's the Tele-set!"

"Hey, there's the Wireless."

"Golly, I wish I had one of those!"

"Hey, I figured it out. At a nickel a week, it'd take you twelve years to get that set. You'd be twenty-six when you got it."

At the far end of the car, a man in a white lab coat held up a small flask. Before the very eyes of his audience, he passed his hand over the tube. Its clear liquid turned a dark burgundy. "Water to wine, boys!" the man proclaimed. Then he passed his other hand over the tube. The wine changed back to water! "Gilbert Chemical Magic, boys. Mystify your friends!"

Ten minutes. Ten minutes was all anyone could linger inside the car. Factory whistles had blown, and the line outside was getting even longer. Kids had to move on. If they wanted to see more, they could come back that evening, when the car would be open from seven-thirty to nine. Stepping out into the muggy afternoon with a free copy of *Erector Tips* in hand, each boy couldn't wait to tell a friend what was inside, and soon what was inside was not much of a surprise. Still, the line refused to shrink as the afternoon wore on. Even though they weren't supposed to, some went through the car twice.

"Hey, you look familiar, kid. Didn't I see you in here an hour ago? Your twin brother, eh? Ah, what the heck. Pick a card, any card."

Toward 5:00 P.M., some kids noticed that the magician, the chemist, and the Erector Man were eyeing each other and checking their watches. Something was about to happen. Would there be prizes? Would Mr. Gilbert appear? Then, as the men suppressed slight smiles, a voice came from a speaker at the rear. "This is radio station WCJ coming to you live from the A. C. Gilbert Company in New Haven, Connecticut." Many of those crammed into the car turned to each other, nudging, listening, beaming. A few had their own crystal sets. Many knew a neighbor who had an actual radio with tubes. Some had never heard a wireless broadcast. The voice sounded so clear as it read the day's headlines, then gave the weather for southern New England. The broadcast lasted just five minutes, but for the rest of the weekend, perhaps the rest of their lives, boys would say they heard their first radio broadcast on the Gilbert Circus Car. And the signal came all the way from New Haven, nearly two hundred miles away.

At 5:30 P.M., the car was closed to visitors. It was empty when a lone man holding a few sheets of paper stepped from the bathroom at the rear. He rubbed his eyes, stretched his legs, then staggered outside for his first gulp of fresh air all afternoon. "Voices through the air," he muttered, followed by an obscenity.

When it first whistle-stopped through New England, the Gilbert Circus Car broadcast live each afternoon from WCJ. But as it roamed south and west, it soon surpassed the limits of radio in 1922. Rather than disappoint children expecting "voices through the air," Gilbert's men decided to play a little trick. Each afternoon, one unlucky stiff was locked in the bathroom with a transcript of the day's WCJ broadcast, wired to Western Union that morning. At the precise hour the station went on the air back at the plant, the broadcaster switched on a microphone and announced the same program. "It wasn't quite honest, of course," Gilbert later admitted, "but it made a wonderful show. And what the kids heard was exactly what went over the air from New Haven—we saw to that. If you could have seen the wide shining eyes of those boys and girls, you wouldn't have deprived them of the thrill for anything."

That evening, the whole show was repeated, with an 8:00 P.M. "broadcast." But under a drizzling rain, the crowd was small. Rather than bring their boys to the Gilbert car, many parents had chosen to attend a meeting at Boys' High School, where a curfew and a possible Boys' Club were being considered to curb incidents of "rowdyism." A few minutes before 9:00 P.M., the car was nearly empty. Then after another tour of downtown, the men staggered back to the car and bunked down in it for the night. On Friday, lines formed again, wireless broadcasts boomed through the car, and boys beamed. That night the men packed the kits and sets, put flags back inside, and prepared to leave town the next morning.

All weekend, beneath the Victorian turrets of Reading's row houses, parents persistently told their children, "No!" No, we can't afford another Erector set. No, your mother doesn't trust you with a chemistry set. What in the world would you want with a Gilbert Hydraulic and Pneumatic Engineering kit? Maybe. We'll see. Ask when it's closer to Christmas. Yet despite such inertia, weekend sales of Gilbert toys rose dramatically in Neubling's and other stores. By then, the Gilbert Circus Car had rolled out of Reading, heading east, bringing toys, science kits, and a "live wireless" broadcast from its own bathroom.

Science and magic lie at opposite ends of the spectrum spanning reason and faith. Science shares its secrets. Magic refuses to reveal them. Science begins with explanation. Magic is destroyed by it. And among the questions that make adults out of the rough clay of childhood are: Which side are you on? Do you *believe* in magic? Or are you one of those kids who can't sleep until you figure out how a trick is really done? Back in the days of Houdini, magic was winning this perennial tug-of-war. Few in Gilbert's audiences in Moscow or New Haven *believed* he could make cards and coins disappear, but they were willing to suspend skepticism for an evening. They enjoyed being gulled. And magic was not the only faith-based show in town. Also popular were séances conducted by spiritualists contacting the dead, "medicine shows" offering miracle cures, and the biggest traveling show of all, the tent revival featuring Billy Sunday or some other evangelist. By the 1920s, however, science had come from behind to pull even. Science triumphed during the 1925 Scopes "Monkey Trial." Although John Scopes was convicted of teaching evolution in Tennessee, the widely publicized spectacle made a mockery of country bumpkins and their "old-time religion." Meanwhile in American homes, science was plugging in and putting down roots.

As science and magic jousted, Gilbert juggled the two. But a look behind the stage shows that he was rooting for science all along. For an afternoon, a Gilbert boy could turn science into trickery, but even if younger children were fooled, older boys saw how. How light was bent by mirrors. How sound traveled. Science might look magical, Gilbert was saying, but it could all be explained. And so, instead of making true believers, he made young skeptics who would not be fooled by the wizardry of the future. They would ask why. They would demand to know how. They would pay no attention to the man behind the curtain, because they had been that man when they were boys.

At least, some of them had. No one knows how many boys bought Gilbert's dazzling array of science kits, but it couldn't have been many. The kits were out of production by 1923. Price may have been to blame; the Weather Bureau sold for $37.50, equivalent to a few hundred dollars today. The Gilbert Civil Engineering set cost $25. Compared to these, the Hydraulic and Pneumatic Engineering kit seemed a bargain at only $15. Still, not enough boys wanted to be hydraulic engineers. There just weren't enough young mineralogists or aspiring glassblowers to make their training tools turn a profit. Yet Gilbert never stopped trying to train young scientists. He kept his chemistry set right through to the company's end, and later added a popular microscope and telescope. Electricity sets came in and out of his line. Radio kits were jazzed up with transistors in the 1950s. But the rest of his science kits became collector's items. Gilbert hadn't foreseen it, but science was already changing, moving beyond the purview of neighborhood magic shows. Surpassing a boy's understanding, science was becoming complex, mystical, even dangerous. "Gee, Dad" was becoming "Why can't I, Mom?" By the mid-1920s, most of Gilbert's science kits would be gone, but for a few years, they continued to ride the rails.

As the summer of 1922 rolled on, the Gilbert Circus Car rolled with it. Out of Reading on July 1, the train headed to Philadelphia for the long Fourth of July weekend. The same morning the train left Reading, a massive nationwide railroad strike began, threatening to delay the march of science. Protesting a wage cut, 400,000 shop men walked off their jobs. Train schedules east of the Mississippi would be disrupted all summer. Many passenger trains were taken out of service. Numerous accidents occurred as strikebreakers fumbled with switches and train routing. Yet the Gilbert Circus Car headed on, south to Wilmington, Baltimore,

and D.C., before moving back across the Appalachians. July 11—
Hagerstown, Maryland. July 12—Chambersburg, Pennsylvania.
July 15—Altoona. July 17—Johnstown. July 18—Greensburg.
July 19 and 20—Pittsburgh. Then Gilbert's car took science and
magic on to Ohio, Michigan, and deeper into the heartland.

7¹⁄₂

The Chapter That Builds the Lift Bridge

The bridge that spanned the narrows separating Washington's Olympic Peninsula from the mainland was light, graceful, and elegant. State-of-the-art engineering when it opened in 1940, it was the twin of the Whitestone Bridge in New York. Its tall towers framed a half mile of two-lane asphalt gently bowed by steel cables. Locals were proud of the new bridge. It wasn't quite the Golden Gate, opened just a few years earlier, but it was easily the most impressive bridge in the Northwest, and the third-longest suspension bridge in the world. Yet the span wasn't open long before drivers noticed something a little shaky about it.

Even in a slight wind, the bridge swayed and buckled. Some began calling it "Galloping Gertie." Adventurous drivers had fun crossing it in high winds. It was like driving on a roller coaster, they said. Then on November 7, 1940, winds whipping through the Tacoma Narrows hit 40 mph. You've seen the footage. Almost everyone has. The Tacoma Narrows Bridge flails in the wind, as if it were the first state-of-the-art suspension bridge built entirely of bubble gum. With one lone car stuck in the center, the steel-and-cement roadway ripples like bedsheets hung out to dry. After only a few minutes, the wind puts the bridge out of its misery. Whole chunks of roadway crash into Puget Sound while smaller strips peel off like bark from a tree, leaving cement shreds dangling from cables. And you can't help but imagine the head engineer addressing his firm the following day: "Well, perhaps for our next bridge, let's try to go beyond 'light, graceful, and elegant.'"

The Tacoma Narrows Bridge haunted me as I contemplated the Lift Bridge I was about to build with my No. 7½ Erector Set. I knew that my own bridge, just three feet long, would not suffer the same stresses, but if paid professionals armed with government contracts could make such a colossal screwup, I could certainly model their incompetence. The Tacoma Narrows collapse claimed only one life—that of a cocker spaniel named Tubby. No life would be at stake on my bridge, yet my status as a role model for my children was at risk. If I built a shaky bridge, how could I preach the gospel of Erector sets or tout engineering as an art form? A lot more than traffic would be riding on my bridge. Those father-child bonds, built of steel yet notoriously flimsy in high winds, were in the offing.

With so much at stake, I took advantage of an Erector feature Gilbert never mentioned. Unlike professional engineers, an Erector builder doesn't have to go public with his work. He can span great waterways and make mighty towers, all in the privacy of his own attic. And once my son lost interest in Erector, just seconds after I took apart our Delivery Truck, that's exactly where I took my set. There in the attic, beneath a single bare bulb, surrounded by cardboard boxes, last year's toys, and busted appliances, I began building my bridge.

As sketched in my manual, the Erector Lift Bridge was scarcely a model of elegance. It consisted of two platforms held aloft by twelve-inch girders on either side. From those towering girders, overhead beams sloped to shorter steel supports on each end. The two identical halves were linked by a flimsy twin arch across the middle. The lift section was a perforated steel platform that rose and fell, powered by a motor bolted onto the towers be-

neath it. To strengthen the bridge, string zigzagged like cables between the roadbed and the girders overhead. The whole contraption resembled a bridge about as much as a preschooler's drawing
of a tree looks like the real thing, yet like Gilbert, I was not striving for verisimilitude. I just wanted to have fun, and to prove myself to the other engineers on the block.

It was peaceful in the attic. I could barely hear the sounds of
a son and daughter at play downstairs. My wife, who was enter-
taining serious doubts about my maturity, had agreed to watch
the kids for an hour. Not bad, I thought, as I plopped my Erector
set on a table. I should do more Erector engineering on a Saturday afternoon in late October. Yet I was not five minutes into my
project when it made me long for a real childhood instead of this
unreasonable facsimile.

The first beams went up without a hitch. The roadway itself
was easy to build, just three screws bolting two plates together.
But then I encountered a classic Erector problem. Many bolts
hold more than one girder. Some have three or four girders fanning out from a single screw and nut. Any beginner who doesn't
notice this ends up unscrewing bolts in order to slip another
girder on them. And another. Like Gilbert, by the time I had built
the first half of my bridge, I felt I had "put together more bolts
and nuts than any man alive or dead," but I didn't have much fun
doing it.

One hour's dedicated work built the first half of the bridge.
This included the little Erector house, painted pale yellow with a
red roof and bolted to one side of the platform. The house didn't
seem to belong on my bridge. On the Fire Lookout, built with
the No. 4½ Erector, the same house was a lookout post. On the
Merry Go-Round, it was the ticket booth. But hanging in midair,
the little steel house made it seem as if someone had taken up residence on the edge of my bridge just to keep an eye on me.
Nonetheless, I bolted the house on and, having used up my family's indulgence, took a last look at my half bridge and went back

to the real world downstairs, the one where things don't fall apart
as often as we think they do. The second half of the project, including motor, gears, and movable parts, would be harder. I
promised myself I'd tackle it soon. I turned off the attic light.

Weeks passed. Months rolled by. Pages fell from the calendar
like so much roadway peeling off a botched bridge. Whenever I
went into the attic—to get storm windows or store another
busted appliance—my half bridge was still standing. Yet I could
not bring myself to finish it. Another hour could easily have been
wangled, yet when you're not under contract, it's easy to put off
till summer the things you could have done in winter. Was I
dodging my fear of failure? Was I afraid of looking too immature
in my wife's eyes or too ham-handed in my son's? Was this my
midlife crisis? *This?* Other men have more fun when they go
middle-aged crazy. They have torrid and tawdry affairs, drive
blood-red convertibles, run with the bulls in Pamplona. Was it
my fate to conquer middle age by building an Erector set bridge
in my attic? Gee, I said, but had nothing more to add.

Finally, I could avoid it no longer. Half a bridge was not better than none. It suggested a middle age half empty, not half full.
So one spring afternoon when no one was in the house, I returned
to the attic and went back to work. Or was it play?

Before tackling the motor assembly, I had to frame the second half of the bridge. That was much easier than the first, being
a mirror image, sans little painted house. Avoiding the mistakes
that required unscrewing and rebolting, I had that baby up in no
time. It was painless, even boring. At its most mundane, building
with an Erector set is like following a recipe. You look carefully
at the drawing and note the next part. Rifling through the red
metal box, you grab a girder and count holes or notches to make
sure you have the exact piece Gilbert had in mind. Then you
count the empty notches up the beam to find where the screw
should be inserted. You bolt it in place, then rifle the box for another girder. Beam by beam, bolt by bolt, count by count, you

match the diagram as if it were some build-by-numbers kit. When all the girders are in place, you're done. And after procrastinating through an entire season, I finished the second half of the bridge in fifteen minutes.

There they were on my attic table. Two half bridges. Each standing tall, proud, begging to be motorized. Now came the acid test. I was about to surpass my own boyhood. The Erector set I had been given in 1961 did not come with a motor, but now I had to install one and rig it to lift a bridge section. Was this when my ineptitude with all things mechanical would reveal itself? Was this where the Tacoma Narrows syndrome would strike? Preparing myself for failure, I rifled through the red box and found the gears, flywheel, and motor needed to make my bridge a genuine lift model.

Bolting on the motor was simple: Count up two holes and over two on each suspension plate. Insert screws. Tighten nuts. A child could do it—perhaps only a child, or a childlike adult. Assembling the elevated roadway was also a cakewalk, just three plates bolted together. Making those plates move, however, was a problem worthy of Washington Roebling. At least the builder of the Brooklyn Bridge had the foresight not to make it a lift bridge. I, however, had chosen to go mobile. And so, step by step, here's how I spent my last ninety minutes as a civil engineer:

1. carefully insert axle into the motor casing
2. suddenly note that unlike the diagram, my axle does *not* have a gear on it
3. yank axle out again, rifle through box, find that damn gear and jam it on
4. wiggle damn gear till it meshes with smaller damn gear beneath it
5. spend ten minutes searching all over attic for flywheel
6. find it on floor beneath manual
7. attach flywheel to axle by tightening its impossibly tiny and torturous set screw

8. swear like a rap artist while struggling to connect flywheel to metal strip on roadway
9. vow to dance on Gilbert's grave in New Haven
10. seconds before storming downstairs to get a sledgehammer, finally attach flywheel to roadway
11. lift bridge overhead as if to heave it upon discovering that flywheel now slams into the axle at each full turn
12. remind myself that temper tantrums set bad example for children
13. find shorter axle and install it while humming "Whistle While You Work"
14. hook some stupid gizmo to some idiotic flange and tighten the bastard
15. link the two halves together by bolting their overhanging arches
16. tell myself I don't need no stinking strings to hold the bridge up—they're clearly cosmetic
17. vow that if I suffer another midlife crisis, I'll go for the blood-red convertible or the torrid, tawdry affair

And then I am finished.

Preparing to take my bridge downstairs, I consider a ribbon-cutting ceremony—some bouffant Miss Erector holding scissors, a mayor making a speech, a band playing a Sousa march. I choose instead to test the motor. Will it even lift? I carry my bridge to the nearest electrical outlet. Lying on the floor in my bedroom, I plug it in. Instantly the motor begins to whir. The gears engage. The flywheel spins. And the roadway rises! And falls. And rises again. And falls. And rises.... What kind of bridge is this, the kind you'd find in a miniature golf course? Would drivers have to time their crossing, flooring it to reach the other side before my bridge sent them plunging off the edge? I yank the plug and examine my model piece by piece. Everything is just as in the drawing. Gears in place. Flywheel as pictured. I plug it in, and again my bridge is not a lift bridge. It's a flapping bridge.

After a few minutes of disgrace, I discover the little metal clutch on my motor. Sliding it to one side, I can disengage the gears and halt the incessant up/down. Timing is of the essence. That must be why mine is the world's only lift bridge with a little house off to one side. The guy who lives there spends his days engaging and disengaging the clutch to keep cars from crashing and suing him for all he's worth. I spend a few minutes perfecting my timing, then take my bridge downstairs to show to my family.

"Nice," my wife says, but her voice suggests she already has two children and sees no need for a third. My daughter's indifference reinforces every gender stereotype Gilbert girls spent decades fighting. My son thinks the bridge is pretty interesting— for about five minutes. He learns to lift it, pause it, lower it. Then he goes back to his Legos, and my bridge goes back in the attic. I have built it. I have been a boy again. Yet I don't feel much like an engineer.

Building the bridge may not have been easy, but neither was it especially creative. Find a girder. Count the holes. Insert a screw. This wasn't engineering, it was general contracting, following a blueprint to the letter. If I really wanted to prove myself an engineer, I'd have to do what Gilbert boys did to enter the Gilbert Institute of Engineering. I'd have to design my own model. But what? From a simple cradle to the Walking Beam Engine, my manual already included every mechanical device from the first half of the twentieth century. And any machine made since 1954 would require far more doohickeys than my set contained. So what could I build?

For another month, I pondered. And during that month, I saw how Gilbert changed the way boys were made.

Every bridge I had once passed unnoticed now commanded my attention. Every machine made me wonder what was inside. I noticed gears. I sensed the tension, fatigue, and stress that a well-made structure is designed to withstand. Before I began building with Erector, tension, fatigue, and stress were forces that added up to a headache. Now they shaped my world. And to that world, although no one asked for it, I would add my own construction. An Eiffel Tower, I decided. Attic-size, handmade, and built without any help from an old manual. So far as I knew, no Gilbert boy was ever stupid enough to try an Erector Eiffel Tower. Mine would be the first. "Pourquoi?" some might ask. My answer: Once we Gilbert boys see how things are put together, building becomes our raison d'être.

> We are all blind until we see,
> That in the human plan,
> Nothing is worth the making,
> If it does not make the man.
>
> Why build these cities glorious,
> If man unbuilded goes?
> In vain we build the world, unless
> The builder also grows.
> —EDWIN MARKHAM

8

The King of Connecticut

Ever since the first king climbed atop the first heap of contenders to the throne, kingdoms have been based on certain keys. Land. Shiny metals. The loyalty of armies. The stooped backs of serfs or slaves. But let history note that during the 1930s, when most Americans could barely spare a dime, Alfred Carleton Gilbert built a kingdom founded on toys.

His was a benevolent realm, its riches shared openly with friends, family, and sometimes with his own employees. It was not the largest personal fiefdom during the Great Depression, yet it lacked few of royalty's trappings. By 1930 the Gilberts were living in a stately fifteen-room Tudor home on Ridge Road in Hamden, just north of New Haven. Gilbert called the home Maraldene, a name he coined by adding the old English suffix *dene*, meaning "house on a hill," to the first syllables of Mary and Alfred. Maraldene had a kennel housing some of the finest German shepherds in the world. Maraldene had separate quarters for its servants, a man-made waterfall, and rooms full of antique English furniture, including a dinner table that, so the story went, once belonged to Oliver Cromwell. Chandeliers were many and varied. In a hallway near the front door, a floor-to-ceiling trophy case gleamed with 150 cups, medals, and plaques from Gilbert's athletic career. White mountain laurel, Connecticut's state flower, billowed from bushes ringing the spacious grounds.

A few miles away, Gilbert had his own 600-acre private hunting estate. Without the slightest touch of irony, he called it Paradise. Paradise's lodge was filled with big-game trophies shot by Gilbert himself. Trout leaped in a pond so close to the lodge that Gilbert could fish for them from his second-story balcony. When leaving his two palaces, this erstwhile king hobnobbed with the likes of General Douglas MacArthur and managed the American Olympic team at the games in Europe and America. He hosted the nation's first weekly sports show, *A. C. Gilbert's Famous Sports Talks,* standing at a microphone and dwarfed by Babe Ruth and other athletes. As his kingdom grew, Gilbert micromanaged it like a modern Peter the Great, hacking trails in Paradise with his own hands, personally thinning his herds of white-tailed deer, and selling off parcels of his land to develop houses. Yet although he seemed the master of all he surveyed, Gilbert was disturbed by a common trap of royalty—a crown prince utterly unlike his father.

Striding toward his fifties, Gilbert was every inch the grown-up Gillie. Time had slowed him, of course, but not by much. He still arose daily at 6:00 A.M., then ran a mile on the dirt roads near Maraldene before returning to his basement gym, where he worked out with Indian clubs and belabored a punching bag. At 7:30 sharp he was at his factory, standing in line and chatting with employees as each, Gilbert included, punched a clock. For as long as he could sit still, Gilbert stayed in his office, meeting with fellow executives, testing new toys, or answering letters. Restless, he then walked around his plant, usually dropping in on his engineers, many of them surrogate sons who shared his interests in magic and toys. Yet as he grew older, he spent more afternoons in Paradise, roaming the grounds with one prize dog or another. Smoking his pipe, he wandered free and unencumbered, yet brooded so much he eventually developed an ulcer. He still did magic when requested, protesting that he was rusty, then amazing people with card tricks and other sleight of hand. Although he was a millionaire many times over, he retained the eccentric stinginess of many self-made men, offsetting it with a common fairness to customers and the employees he called his "coworkers."

"A. C.," he was often told at meetings, "you gotta raise the price on those small tool chests. We can't sell 'em for $1.98. We're losing a buck on every one." Again and again, Gilbert refused. "Make up the loss somewhere else," he'd say, adding that he wanted bottom-dollar toys for boys who could afford no better. At such meetings, he would often sit back and put his shoes on his desk, shoes that usually had a hole in the sole. When he didn't come to the factory in his hunting gear—old pants, boots, a flannel shirt—he wore a tattered suit that belied his worth. An official of the Amateur Athletic Union, of which Gilbert was a director, recalled seeing him at an AAU convention one year in a threadbare coat with a prominent black spot, most likely burned by the lit pipe he often stuck absentmindedly in his pocket. "I didn't pay much attention to it at the time," the man recalled, "but there he was at the next convention—same coat, same burn." If he needed new clothes, Gilbert usually ordered them from L. L. Bean, back when Bean sold no preppy attire, just practical outdoor garb.

Though balding and aged by wrinkles that betrayed his few legible emotions, Gilbert retained the "practical boy psychology" that had made his fortune. *Erector Tips* had been discontinued in 1922, yet his ads still spoke to boys as best friends. "Hello Boys! The boy who gets my new TRAILBLAZING NO. 8 ERECTOR for Christmas will sure be the talk of the town. When you've built your 5-foot model of a real trans-Atlantic

Zeppelin, your pals will flock from miles around to look it over. . . . Now boys, here's the way to get this barrelful of red blooded fun. . . ." And Gilbert still loved a good promotional stunt, even at home. One Christmas afternoon, children all along Ridge Road were startled to see a plane overhead. This was shortly after Lindbergh's famous flight, and planes were still rare sightings. The plane circled over a golf course, did some barrel rolls, then climbed to 1,500 feet. On the ground, hands pointed to *something* that had bailed out of it. Seconds later, a parachute opened. As it descended, the chutist was seen to be wearing a red suit. While children came running, the jumper landed in a clump of trees on Gilbert's estate, shouting, "Ho, ho, ho!" Soon, this skydiving Santa Claus, hired by Gilbert, was passing out presents to seventeen-year-old Charlotte Gilbert, eleven-year-old Lucretia, nine-year-old Al Jr., and their friends.

As his business mushroomed, Gilbert added to his factory until it sprawled across twenty-one buildings served by a seven-track railroad spur. Yet he retained a quaint, small-time management style. Among the specimens in each of his microscope sets were dead flies he had electrocuted by wiring fences near the barn in Paradise. Gilbert insisted that the bright red paint used on Erector boxes be carefully matched to that of a cocktail shaker he kept on his desk. And whenever packaging was upgraded, Gilbert had one of his engineers throw boxes of Erector and chemistry sets down the three flights of stairs behind his office to see if the new packages would protect them. If a set could survive that tumble, he figured, it could make it to San Francisco by rail.

No matter how eccentric he became, however, Gilbert knew what boys wanted. In 1924, after his Circus Car no longer seemed novel, Gilbert turned the bulk of his energy toward Erector. In the free-spending Jazz Age, more parents could splurge, so Gilbert gave them Erector sets to fill a big boy's fantasy. Top sets had tipped the scales at thirty-two pounds, but now they started gaining weight in a hurry. In the first year of expansion, the biggest set weighed fifty-four pounds. Two years later it was beefed up to sixty-eight pounds. Then eighty pounds. By 1931, the No. 10, filling a box eight inches thick and nearly three feet by two feet, contained 150 pounds of gears, rods, axles, brackets, base plates, boilers, hooks, cranks, strips, pulleys, wheels, propellers, bells, tires, springs, cams, washers, nuts, bolts, and girders. There was hardly a contraption you couldn't assemble with all this paraphernalia; the manual pictured 500 models. But these enormous sets were not just rattling boxes of random parts. Each made one special model that put the energy of the era into a boy's hands.

Building big was the tenor of the times. While Gilbert was creating Maraldene and Paradise, American industry was capping an age of muscular engineering whose structures still make us gawk. Riding a roller coaster from prosperity to depression, engineers built the Chrysler Building (1930), the Empire State Building (1931), and hotels with one, two, and three thousand rooms. They built Hoover Dam (1935) and the Golden Gate Bridge (1937). And they poured enough concrete into Washington's Grand Coulee Dam (finished in 1942) to build a six-foot-wide sidewalk all the way around the equator. Building these behemoths, workers dangled from cables and balanced on beams surrounded by sky. The lone builder became the symbol of modern man—an antlike creature erecting structures that made him feel either inspired or insignificant, depending on the time of day. America was also accelerating, getting around in cars, trucks, planes, boats, and blimps, so each enormous Erector set built its own model of modern transportation.

A truck as long as a little sister. A Ferris wheel as sturdy as Lou Gehrig. A cigar-shaped zeppelin just like the amazing German airships crossing the Atlantic—the *Graf Zeppelin* and the largest object yet airborne, the *Hindenburg*. Erector's zeppelin was framed by girders, then covered in a white canvas bag stamped with the red-and-gold Erector logo. Like some long white cigar, the airship hung from the ceiling beneath a bracket that let it circle overhead, while far below on the floor, its maker pondered what to build next. A steam shovel? A working print-ing press? Maybe even an Eiffel Tower?

More special models were in store each year. In 1929, when Gilbert bought out his longtime rival, Meccano, his Meccano-Erector sets made a steel ocean liner that really sailed! And then there was the Hudson Locomotive. Like buildings and bridges, real-life locomotives had grown to gargantuan scale. The largest had wheels eight feet tall and a cab as high as a second-story win-dow. From it an engineer gazed across an engine over one hun-dred feet long and weighing a million pounds. Steaming through small towns, these locomotives shook the earth for a block in all directions. Boys putting pennies on the tracks—whoa! flat as a pancake!—couldn't help but want their own models, so Gilbert obliged. His 1931 No. 10 assembled a replica of New York's Twentieth Century Limited. Four feet long, black and silver, with art deco design, the Hudson Locomotive was the most coveted Erector model. It had nowhere to run, no tracks big enough to hold it. Yet put up on blocks to let the wheels spin, it sure lit up a boy's room. There was no other word for it but "Jeepers!"

These special models earned Erector its slogan "The World's Greatest Toy." And well-to-do parents paid the world's greatest toy prices for them, coughing up $60, even $70, at a time when a tin soldier cost a penny and $70 would buy a cheap used car. Soon Erector's many options inspired Gilbert to name his sets instead of just numbering them. In the christening, he was characteristi-cally boyish and blunt. The No. 1 became "The Dandy Begin-ner's Set." No. 3 was "The Set with the Big Red Wheels." No. 10 became "The Complete, Unsurpassable Erector in All Its Glory." These were not toys; they were apprentice tools. Pushing the up-per edge of boyhood, they were aimed at boys who today would be called young men. The sixteen-, seventeen-, and eighteen-year-olds who mastered these sets had taken their last step before land-ing that first paying job in a tool and die shop or heading on to college. Throughout the era of muscular engineering, Gilbert's grandest sets let bigger boys design the meatiest Erector models ever and win the biggest prizes. In 1935 Oliver Henry Fulton of Pittsburgh built a Cement Mixer and Distributing Crane. The crane rotated, swiveled, and ran a bucket along its track. As big and bulky as his mother's icebox, the structure earned Fulton first prize in Gilbert's annual contest—a free trip to Hollywood, or $500. Fulton took the money and used it toward his tuition at MIT, where he earned a bachelor's degree in physics in 1940.

Once Gilbert's toys and the regal life they provided him drew wide attention, he was mythologized in the popular press. His story seemed scripted according to the American dream, yet journalists still felt the need to embellish it. Article after article spun stories, saying that Gilbert, like Charles Atlas, who was then starting his bodybuilding empire, had been a ninety-seven-pound weakling. Young Gilbert, one magazine wrote, was a "physically handicapped lad, not strong and healthy as most boys are. Rather he was thin, frail, and undersized." Yet with luck and pluck, he built himself into an Olympic gold medalist. (The awkward truth about his having to share the medal was conveniently ignored.) Medal in hand, the mythical Gilbert set out to conquer his next obstacle—poverty. Before turning his simple idea into a fortune, *Forbes* noted, he and Mary had lived on just $60 a month. One newspaper headlined Gilbert's story "Pole Vault from Poverty." Such fictions lived on until Gilbert refuted them in his 1954 autobiography, *The Man Who Lived in Paradise.* By then the myth had been repeated in *Life,* the *New Yorker, Reader's Digest,* the *Wall Street Journal, Believe It or Not,* and Dale Carnegie's syndicated column.

The press could make Gilbert larger than life, but nothing could make him settle down. As the money poured in, he poured it out on hobbies that met his need for control, mastery, and competition. He tried golf for a while but, although he often approached par, gave it up because "I've decided I can't master the game." While visiting Erector's plant in Austria, Gilbert was introduced to German shepherds. He had always owned dogs—from a cocker spaniel in Oregon to a bulldog at Yale—but none had touched him like this breed. Within a few years, Maraldene Kennels boasted the nation's top shepherds, each with a proud German name and a lengthy pedigree. Noble, high-strung, and trained to understand a hundred commands, these champions were to ordinary dogs as kings are to commoners. One of Gilbert's favorites was Asta von Kaltenweide, three-time German champ and second only to the celebrated Rin Tin Tin in honors and fame. After Asta won the coveted Max von Stephanitz Award (named for the man who created the breed), Gilbert refused an offer of $12,000 for her, nearly twice what he'd paid. Instead he mated her with another favorite, Alf von Tollensetal. For Gilbert, these dogs were more than breeders; they were friends. Alf sat by Gilbert's chair every evening while he pored over business journals and was his constant companion outside. The dog romped with his children and delighted them when Gilbert, while Mary was away one night, ordered Alf into his bed the next morning, pretending he'd slept with the dog all night. Gilbert would later say of Alf and other favorites that no human ever understood him as well.

Gilbert ran his own kennel for a dozen years but came to loathe dog shows, where he found the people "jealous and petty." He continued to have dogs in Paradise but turned his attention to another breed of thoroughbred—the amateur athlete. These days, the name Yale suggests scholars and scientists, but in the 1920s and '30s, the university was also known for its pole vaulters. Year after year, Yale vaulters won national championships. Gilbert was one reason. As the first man to clear thirteen feet, he coached the first man to clear fourteen feet, and also worked with other world record holders. "A. C. Gilbert knows more about pole vaulting than any other man in the world," a rival track coach said. *Encyclopaedia Britannica* editors agreed, hiring Gilbert to write the encyclopedia's article on the event. Too old to demonstrate his technique, Gilbert passed it on through modeling and movies. While judging collegiate meets, he shot slow-motion film of vaulters. At the start of each track season, he invited Yale vaulters to Maraldene. After dinner, Gilbert put on a clinic, demonstrating a small device he had built to model the physics of vaulting, then showing his movies. For the rest of the season, Gilbert spent a couple hours every afternoon at the track. His expertise soon earned him a position on the American Olympic Committee and a chance to return to the games.

In 1928 Gilbert accompanied General Douglas MacArthur, then head of the American Olympic Committee, to the games in Amsterdam. While other members of the delegation played and partied, Gilbert and the general were all business. MacArthur gave stirring speeches; Gilbert worked as the team's morale officer. Decades later, Gilbert was puzzled when MacArthur was relieved of his command. "He was a fine man," Gilbert recalled of the general whose bravado made Caesar look spineless, "and I have never been able to understand the charges leveled against him that he was egotistical." In Amsterdam, Gilbert watched proudly as his Yale protégé Sabin Carr won the pole vault. Four years later, Gilbert managed the American team at the games in Los Angeles. He was eager to do the same in Berlin, but some argued that the United States should boycott the 1936 Olympics in protest of Hitler's racial policies. Gilbert disagreed. The integrated American team would make Germany's youth see that "the pronouncements of their government were not quite so sound as they had been led to believe," he told the press. When Jesse Owens won four gold medals, the crowd chanted his name, Hitler stormed out of the stadium, and Gilbert was vindicated. Though he never met the führer, he and other American officials were feted by propaganda minister Joseph Goebbels. The following year, the Third Reich sent Gilbert a special Olympic medal and certificate, signed by Hitler himself. Gilbert kept it as a souvenir, even though he would soon retool his factory to fight fascism.

While Gilbert pursued excellence, his company struggled to stay solvent in an economy verging on 25 percent unemployment. Coming from the old school of business, Gilbert was reluctant to borrow money, so as the depression deepened, he scaled back. His entire workforce, including Gilbert himself, took 10 percent pay cuts for two straight years. In 1933, with sales plummeting, Erector became child-size again. The enormous sets and special models were discontinued, leaving muscular engineering to men. Still, Gilbert's company floundered. Its stock fell from $25 to $2 a share. Yet Gilbert's good name kept his from being one of nearly a hundred toy companies that closed shop during the 1930s. By mid-decade the company was turning a small profit, and it soon returned to annual sales of $2 million. Meanwhile, the king of Connecticut enlarged his realm. Just before the crash, Gilbert had sold half his company stock for $1.25 million. He put this in gilt-edged securities that allowed him to live nobly. He sent his son to Phillips Andover Academy. He expanded Paradise, planting 700 apple trees, adding seven ponds, twenty bridges, and a herd of Jersey cattle, which, he noted in his relentless competitive spirit, was rated one of the nation's top dairy herds. Even as he made his estate more utopian, however, he could not recapture his boyhood there. To do that, he had to roam farther from Paradise.

Some of Gilbert's fondest memories came from camping trips with his father in the Cascades. When he settled in southern New England, where so-called mountains are really hills and the wildest game is raccoon, he shelved his love of the outdoors. But after hunting duck and quail on his own estate, he longed for big skies and mountains to match his manhood. So in the midst of the depression he headed west again, loaded for bear. After crossing the country by train, he and a friend took a stagecoach and a pack train to reach Kimberley, British Columbia. Then they set out on foot over Summit Pass and down through the Canadian Rockies toward White Swan Lake. The trip was a fiasco. Gilbert's morning jogs had not prepared him for hiking in knee-deep snow at several thousand feet. He was also a few months early for hunting season. He was swept into rushing creeks and crippled by leg cramps. He missed the only bear he got in his sights, yet he fell in love with the snowcapped country where moose, elk, and big-horn sheep were spotted more often than humans. Sleeping in a tepee and waking each morning to salmon sunrises over crystal blue lakes, he again emulated his hero. And like Teddy Roosevelt, Gilbert embodied that strange paradox of naturalist and hunter, standing in awe of big game one moment, shooting it the next.

Until his legs would no longer carry him, Gilbert returned to the Canadian Rockies whenever the urge struck him. And since he and Mary by then lived together but in separate spheres, the urge struck him often. He built a cabin on White Swan Lake, eighty miles from the nearest road or railroad. He often flew with bush pilots into the wilds of Alaska. Exploring the backcountry for weeks at a time, he and his hunting buddies lived like moun-tain men. Photos show Gilbert bent over a camping stove wear-ing a plaid hunting shirt, suspenders, and a floppy hat, a stubbled, grubby hobo, free and content. With practice, Gilbert became a skilled big-game hunter, winning several national prizes. He bagged nearly every large North American mammal, including some of the biggest bears ever mounted. Most of his trophies were sent home to Paradise, whose lodge came to resemble a child's daydream of Daniel Boone's camp. The two-story log cabin was jammed with 300 heads—mountain lion, bobcat, bald eagle, caribou, wolverine, musk ox, walrus, polar bear, antelope, timber wolf, lynx, and more. Huge bear rugs lined each floor. Enormous grizzlies, jaws agape, leered from quiet corners. Even with three large fireplaces and comfy chairs, the lodge must have been a hard place to sleep. Yet Paradise was not just Gilbert's pri-vate hideaway. Each fall, when the Army-Navy game was played at the Yale Bowl, Gilbert hosted generals and admirals there. He brought clients by to talk business and shoot quail. He also rented Paradise to hunting parties for $225 a weekend. In their letters, hunters thanked him for the great time—"a man isn't en-titled to have that much fun"—often adding that someone in the party had left his shoes somewhere in the lodge.

Among the guests at Paradise was one who would help

Gilbert win even more boys. W. O. Coleman ostensibly came to Paradise to hunt deer, but he had an ulterior motive. By 1937 Coleman's company, American Flyer, was about to become another victim of hard times. Wouldn't the nation's most famous grown-up boy want to buy his own model train company? "I was interested, of course," Gilbert recalled. "Who isn't interested in electric trains?" Yet he balked at taking on more debt. Only when Coleman offered him American Flyer with no money down and a mere promise of royalties did Gilbert acquire the company and begin to revive it. First he patented a device that said "choo choo!" as engines chugged around the track. Joshua Lionel Cowen's trains couldn't do that! Then, like any boy with trains, Gilbert imagined a layout. Whole cities and switchyards. Papier-mâché mountains with tunnels. Crisscrossing tracks and bridges. Being Gilbert, he wanted to share his new toys with every boy on every block, and sell a few million. So in the spring of 1941 he leased a seven-story building in Manhattan at the triangle formed by Broadway and Fifth Avenue near West Twenty-fifth Street. He hired designers to create elaborate indoor displays. Outdoors, he put up a 150-foot-long sign proclaiming "Gilbert Hall of Science." And in September of that year, he gave the hall to the boys and girls of America.

On opening day, 1,500 kids spilled over the sidewalk and onto the street. Flocking around the building, they clamored to see through eight large portholes. Each looked in on something out of a wish list—an Erector Parachute Jump modeled after the ride at the New York World's Fair, shiny microscopes and chemistry sets, and trains, trains, trains! At 10:00 A.M., a Boy Scout fife-and-drum corps struck up a tune. Scouts saluted as a stern police officer introduced the man whose name was on the building. Gilbert seemed genuinely cheerful that day, even smiling. He called his new hall "a dream come true" that would lead "the young and struggling chemist, constructionist, railroad builder, scientist and research worker, to the goal that is success." Taking keys from his burned pocket, Gilbert handed them to a young man chosen to represent "all boys everywhere." This very adult-looking adolescent opened the doors. The crowd streamed inside.

The hall's first floor was filled with Erector, all the sets laid out for boys to see and covet. Touch a button labeled "Push Me," and the biggest models came to life, gyrating, lifting, and loading. Flanking the sets were science displays. Touch another button, and snapping sparks rose up two metal prongs. Push a third button, and a metal ring leaped from one tilted bar to another. Boys who could tear themselves away turned to face a giant locomotive towering to the ceiling. This was the information desk. Everywhere a boy looked, there were Mysto magic sets, telescopes, girders galore, and free engineers' caps for all.

Upstairs was an entire floor filled with trains. Tracks looped through a world of railroads keener than any boy could hope to own. On an eighty-foot-long diorama, nine trains zipped and chugged. In one section, two hurtled toward each other, about to collide. At the last second, a semaphore turned red, stopping one train, letting the other chug past. After ogling the trains, boys dying to own American Flyer or any other Gilbert toy dragged a parent to the third-floor salesroom. There, women with bright lipstick and dull smiles radioed orders to the basement, where the toys were packed and brought to the front desk.

On the fourth floor, Gilbert sold his appliances. There were never many boys on that floor.

Toys were the hall's attraction, but seen through the porthole of old photos, the boys themselves seem more interesting. Some in scout uniforms, others in sailors' caps, dutifully lining up to push buttons, they seem like boys Gilbert engineered for the occasion. Outside of Norman Rockwell paintings, you don't see many boys like this anymore. Their representative, sixteen-year-old Robert "Bobby" Galagher, who took the keys from Gilbert, carried himself like a college man. He had already toured South America as "boy ambassador," and one suspects that he did not flinch at being called a boy. Yet when Gilbert handed Bobby the

keys and dedicated the hall "to the boys and girls of America forever," neither of the two suspected how short forever would be.
Boys, it seemed, were changing. Had Gilbert chosen to notice, he
could have seen the change in his own son.

It is never easy being the child of a willful and famous man. The
burden is harder still on a son branded with the father's name.
Some sons meet this fate by shadowing their old man's career—
becoming a military officer, a CEO, even the president of the
United States. Others openly rebel, shunning success, living in
communes instead of penthouses, making long lists of their fathers' sins. Alfred Carleton Gilbert Jr. took the former track. Little is known of his childhood, other than the fact that he had all
the Erector sets a boy could want. Born in 1919, he reached the
age of "Gilbert boy" during the era of the huge sets. He grew up
surrounded by the opulence of Maraldene, with occasional visits
to Paradise. It might be expected that his father, having dedicated
his career to boys, would be a model parent. Hadn't he written to
Mary that he hoped to be as good a father "as my father has been
to me"? And yet he was usually too busy. When Al was young,
Gilbert belonged to more than a dozen clubs, committees, bank
boards, and trade groups. The Gilberts always ate dinner together, and then, at bedtime, the father read to his children or told
them the Brer Rabbit stories Frank Gilbert had told him. Every
so often Gilbert and his children spent the night in a log cabin on
the edge of Maraldene, imagining themselves pioneers. But for
the most part, Gilbert, like nearly every father of his time, left the
child raising to his wife. Men who maintain such a dignified distance are often puzzled at how little their children take after
them.

   Al Gilbert was less a "Gilbert boy" than the thousands who
wrote his father every day. He cared nothing for sports. He did
not enjoy hunting and never accompanied his father on his Canadian and Alaskan trips. Though he doubtless saw his father make

coins and cards disappear, he showed no interest in magic, nor did he take to kennels or competition for its own sake. Al's first love was music—something his father rarely listened to. A good drummer, Al also played the trombone, two pursuits that made his parents appreciate Maraldene's many remote rooms. Given a different birthright, Al's friends say, he might have become a musician. Yet like a true scion, Al Gilbert saw where his father's footsteps were leading, so he devised ways of keeping his musical passion at bay. While at Yale, Al spent much of his weekly allowance on records. His tastes ranged from Benny Goodman to classical. Each Sunday, when he came to Maraldene for dinners where the whole family gathered, Al had to present an expense account to his dad. He always waited until 7:00 P.M., after A. C. had enjoyed his favorite radio program, *The Jack Benny Show.* Then he handed over the account, hoping his father, having laughed at Benny's stinginess, would not ask about the largest item on the account—miscellaneous—in which Al had hidden his record purchases.

The younger Gilbert studied engineering at Yale. Unlike his father, he was a top student, graduating with high honors, first in his class. A. C. often worried to friends that his son might be "an intellectual." To dispel such fears, Al also made the Yale swim team, but his lackluster career only increased the distance between king and prince. "It was pretty frustrating," Al once remarked. "I'd be particularly proud of some grades I'd got, and I'd show them to Dad, and he'd say 'Uh-huh. How was swimming today?' I got my major letter in swimming, by sheer work and strife, to please my father." Of this distance, the elder Gilbert said only, "There wasn't much interest in water sports out West when I was growing up."

When Al graduated in 1941, his father encouraged him to seek work at another company "because I thought that a son should start out working for someone other than his own father." The A. C. Gilbert Company was already gearing up for military production, and after Pearl Harbor the plant converted entirely to making war matériel, including machine gun parts, flares, parachutes, and triggers for mines and booby traps. Al spent World War II as an engineer with General Electric. Then in 1946, married and a father of one, with A. C. Gilbert III on the way, he joined the family business as assistant to the president, aka, Dad. There was some resentment among the company's top brass, but Al, personable and obviously qualified, soon dispelled any fears of rank nepotism. He worked his way up the ladder's top rungs, becoming company secretary, then financial vice president, treasurer, and, when A. C. stepped down in 1954, president. In his autobiography, Gilbert lauds his son's efforts and expertise. Yet the book's list of "Notable Events in the Life of A. C. Gilbert" neglects to mention either his marriage or the births of his children. These events couldn't compete with Gilbert's pole-vaulting records, club memberships, and new product lines.

Fulfilling his patrimony, Al Gilbert followed his father, even becoming president of the Toy Manufacturers of America. "Al followed in A. C.'s shoes, but those shoes pinched him a little," said Al's Yale roommate Angus Gordon. "I'm afraid Al failed to recognize how proud of him his father was. But they were so different. A. C. was an Olympic champion, hunter, businessman, not an intellectual, certainly. He saw the outstanding work Al did in school, and it impressed him. Yet Al wasn't so sure. It was an internal pressure he put on himself. He was always wondering, 'Does Dad approve of me?' not so much in the business sense but in the sense of winning a gold medal."

When family and friends look back at the Gilberts, they speak only of the surface. Mary Gilbert was "kind," "generous," "a real lady." A. C. was "very impressive," "decent," "a real gentleman." Probe deeper, and ripples form. A. C. and his son were "not close." A. C. and his brother had "serious tension," which led to A. C. firing F. W. for vague reasons. Dare to dive into these waters, and you crack your head. You suspect a false bottom, that there must be more beneath the rippled surface. The Gilberts, however, were a family, one that gathered every Sunday for dinner. At the head of the table was the quintessential self-made man. No chips could come from his block because he built it from the hardest marble. If father was different from son, then this was the way it was in many families. If the daughters grew up fulfilling their roles as wives and mothers, then anything more must remain the family's affair. Families that meet every week for dinner learn this much about each other—they don't always get along, but what's family remains family. These waters may not run deep, but they run silently.

By the time Al joined his father's company, the Gilbert family at Erector Square was quite extended. Employment peaked at 2,500 in the early 1950s, yet Gilbert continued to treat his "coworkers" as if they were working in a small shop. Turning sheets of steel into toys was anything but imaginative work. Gilbert's factory floor hummed and pounded with casting, pressing, and punching machines. Yet in nurturing his larger family, Gilbert was both personal and creative. A die-hard conservative who hated unions as much as he hated taxes, Gilbert kept the former at bay by treating his workers better than any union might have. Typically, he saw this as a competition: "What the unions have got to prove is that they can do a better job for these people than I can. It's a contest—I'm matched against them—and I win if I can do the better job, which I can."

Gilbert's may have been routine factory work, but it was no sweatshop. It paid prevailing wages, enhanced by remarkable benefits. Long before such things became widespread, Gilbert's coworkers received Blue Cross coverage for $10 a week. Workers were entitled to free medical and legal advice. A half century before Congress passed the Family Leave Act, coworkers who became pregnant were given up to a year's leave of absence. And then there were the perks. The cafeteria often showed movies at lunchtime, and each Friday an orchestra played while coworkers danced. Longtime employees were treated to annual service dinners. For a few years, until the state ruled it was a violation of zoning laws, Gilbert converted part of Paradise into Paradise Park, a private country club open to all coworkers and their families on Sundays and holidays. Membership was $1.50 a year. Above all, Gilbert worked to keep things small, personal, and precise. Each new employee was given a handbook of "Creeds, Policies, and Procedures." It ran to eighty-nine pages. Lest the handbook seem impersonal, Gilbert offered a chivalric benefit to each coworker with five or more years on the job. On their birthdays, men received a boutonnière, women a corsage. And both got a handshake from Gilbert, who, even when half his employees had been there ten years or more, knew every one on a first-name basis. Gilbert even took the trouble to visit the night shift once a week, usually Thursdays, wandering around the floor for a few hours because he worried that the night shift might feel neglected.

Comfortable with their boss, Gilbert's coworkers were rarely tempted by unions. Once when nine men in his print shop joined the printer's union, Gilbert was disillusioned. He seemed to take the move personally. He called the men into his office and gave them a pep talk about team spirit. The men soon voted six-to-three to quit the union. Gilbert was pleased, but a letter from a young woman at the close of World War II meant more to him. "Dear Mr. Gilbert," it read. "I am one of the girls from the Paint Shop and I want to say that I have enjoyed every minute I spent in our plant. It is one of the nices [*sic*] places I have ever been in. I just know it is just as hard for you to lay us off as much as we hated to leave such a swell factory. I believe I speak for all of the girls when I say Thank You Mr. Gilbert for letting us in your plant. . . . It is the best factory in the country. From One of the Happy Gilbert Family, Miss Alberta Linsley, West Haven."

With his contented coworkers, his dutiful crown prince, his prize dogs, and his regal estate, Gilbert reigned until age caught up with him. For longer than usual, however, age too bowed to his will.

In 1950 Gilbert went to Unimak Island on the Aleutian Peninsula, 700 miles southwest of Anchorage. His mission: to bring back a Kodiak bear—dead, of course—for Yale's Peabody Museum of Natural History. A seaplane dropped Gilbert, a guide, and a cook on a lake near the southern edge of the mountainous island, where hunting had never before been permitted. Alone amid the snow-crested peaks, they did not wait long for company. Late on their second afternoon, one "Brownie," as Gilbert called the bears, was spotted across the lake. Deciding it was too late to stalk him, the hunters had dinner. While they were at their campfire, the bear loped around the lake and approached. Gilbert went to the tent to get his gun. Figuring the bear was behind a nearby sand dune, he ran up its side and stood sixty yards from the beast. He fired. The bear took off toward the lake. Gilbert ducked around the dune and missed a few times. The bear reached the water. Gilbert jammed a bamboo staff in the dirt, rested his gun on it, and took one last shot. Gilbert had his museum trophy, if he could get all 1,000 pounds of it out of the lake, onto a plane, and back to Connecticut.

In an inflatable raft, Gilbert and his guide headed out on the lake in the twilight. They got a rope around the bear just before it sank. As darkness fell, they walked through the icy water, sometimes up to their shoulders, wrestling the bear back to shore. They landed him, somehow loaded him onto the bush pilot's plane when it returned, and brought the trophy back to the Peabody Museum, where it still stands in the North American Hall. Visitors gazing up at the enormous bear, eight feet nine inches tall, would have a hard time believing it was brought home by a five-foot-seven, 140-pound man, then sixty-six, whose day job was creating toys.

The Peabody expedition was one of Gilbert's last hunting trips. He returned to his beloved wilderness a few more times, hunting with a camera instead of a gun. He shot many reels of film, which he edited into silent documentaries with melodramatic subtitles: "In the midst of her quiet beauty, Alaska's sharp

temper suddenly breaks forth as the rude storm clouds of a willi-
waw form and race towards us across the angry lake." He
showed these movies in his cafeteria, his lodge, and to local service clubs. But when he retired in 1954, Gilbert began to age rapidly. The following year, when he gave the commencement
address at his alma mater, Pacific University in Oregon, even students who had owned Erector sets must have seen him as an ancient mariner.

Gilbert called the honorary degree he received that day "the
greatest honor that has ever been bestowed upon me." He then
spoke about "Teamwork in Action," sharing his lifelong principles. Chief among them was enthusiasm. "The enthusiastic man
and woman are hill climbers," he said. "They are ever moving upward. They are brushing obstacles aside like so much chaff."
Graduates listened politely, but it was May 1955. Off in the
corner of pop culture, a song entitled "Rock Around the Clock"
was rising toward No. 1 on the charts. The song came from that
spring's hit movie, *Blackboard Jungle,* featuring juvenile delin-
quents at war with their teacher. Was "the boy problem" returning with a vengeance? Or was some other new creature slouching
toward adolescence? Something was in the air, something that
would change boys forever. And to the class of '55, the platitudes
of this man who had been their age a half century earlier—enthusiasm, cooperation, teamwork—sounded like the prattle of a king
whose time was rapidly passing.

The Incredible Shrinking Boy

According to *The Random House Dictionary of American Slang*, the word *nerd* was first used in 1950. It was coined by Dr. Seuss. Among the menagerie of whimsical creatures the good doctor invented in *If I Ran the Zoo* were a Preep, a Proo, a Nerkle, and a Nerd.

Zookeepers paid no attention, but teenagers took notice. Or perhaps they noticed Edgar Bergen's Mortimer Snerd and adapted *nerd* from that dummy. Whichever route the word took to reach the street, it fit a certain type. By the time Elvis reshaped teenage masculinity, the *Oxford English Dictionary* defined *nerd* as "a square." Over the next few years, the word got around, but because teens rarely consult the *OED*, its spelling flip-flopped between *nurd* and *nerd.* Then in 1965, *Time* noted, "At the University of North Carolina, last year's *fink* is this year's *squid, cull, troll,* or *nerd.*" The spelling was fixed. The definition continued to float.

When I was in high school in the late 1960s, a nerd was closely related to a grind, a kiss-ass, or a suck—i.e., some loser who studied a lot. We sucks favored English classes, yet nerds were more often found in physics and calculus. Nerd, it seemed, was evolving toward the definition that has reigned ever since.

Again, *The Random House Dictionary of American Slang:* "**nerd.**
2. an over diligent student; *(hence)* a person obsessively devoted
to a (usu. specified) nonsocial activity." In other words, someone
who actually *likes* math, science, and engineering.

Since the 1970s, *nerd* has spread through pop culture like a
computer virus. Boys and men whom nature made the polar opposite of "cool" have been dogged by the label. The nerd was
mocked in commercials and films *(Revenge of the Nerds).* The
nerd was the guy—always a guy—who wore horn-rimmed
glasses when no one else did. The nerd stayed up late, alone, in
the computer lab long before computers learned how to be cool.
In his pocket, he carried a plastic pen holder, sometimes called a
"nerd pack." The nerd was a walking antifashion statement. You
wouldn't wear *those* pants—they're nerdy. You wouldn't want
your sister to date *that* nerd. Yet somehow, you always ended up
working for some nerd. But another definition for nerd might be
"a former Gilbert boy."

Thirty years before the birth of the nerd, Gilbert assured
boys that science and engineering were the keys to social status:
"The boy who knows about different kinds of engineering . . . is
the type of boy who will be a leader among his fellow boy
friends. He is the boy whom the rest of the boys look up to." It
may never have been entirely so, except in Gilbert's idealized
boyhood. Yet by the time he died in 1961, Gilbert's paradigm of
leadership had been upended. Depending on the high school,
leaders were not future engineers; they were jocks, glad-handed
young politicians, or the guys who had the best cars. Only fellow
nerds looked up to boys who knew about "different kinds of engineering." The rest looked at them with scorn, dismay, or pity. If
boys still respected "a knowledge of different things which they
don't understand," the most coveted field of expertise was not
science but sex. And in their final years on the market, the Gilbert
toys that had once fascinated boys well into their teens were rou-
tinely shunned by boys older than twelve. What had the gods of
pop culture wrought?

The change that turned the "wide-awake" Gilbert boy into a candidate for nerdhood did not occur overnight. There was no 1776 in the process, no war, uprising, or other turning point. The anti-intellectual drift that made science "square" and drastically shortened boyhood was gradual. Its founding fathers were an unlikely mix. They ranged from TV's Fonzie to Felix the Cat's professorial friend Poindexter, from the makers of the first hot rods to the makers of the atomic bomb, and from Albert Einstein to Frankenstein. By fits and starts, the shift paralleled the final three decades of Gilbert's life. It transformed him from the nation's leading boy booster into an archaic old man who, in the mid-1950s, noted that his "old fashioned ideals . . . sound pretty naïve in this cynical day." The revolution was well under way by then, but it had begun during the height of Erector in all its unsurpassed glory.

The same year Gilbert produced his biggest Erector set, audiences lined up outside the Mayfair Theatre in Times Square during a cold December drizzle. They had come to see a new movie based on a classic British novel. It was 1931 and the depression had made audiences ripe for any kind of cinematic escape—the zany antics of the Marx Brothers, the quips of W. C. Fields, even (gasp!) sheer horror. Drawn by Universal Pictures' publicity slogan—"To see it is to wear a badge of courage!"—the Mayfair's opening-night audience paid 35 cents a ticket and filed dutifully into its seats. The lights went down, but before the credits rolled, a man stepped onscreen to deliver a warning. Speaking in a pinched German accent, he began, "How do you do. Mr. Carl Laemmle feels it would be a little unkind to present this picture without a word of warning. We are about to unfold the story of Frankenstein, a man of science." When the film began, many in the audience must have wondered about that warning. There seemed nothing especially shocking about a scientist neglecting his fiancée in favor of his "experiments." That was what scientists did, didn't they? But then science became sinister. Cut to a laboratory on a dark and stormy night. Sparks shoot from electrical apparatus. A mad scientist and his semihuman assistant scurry around a table containing the "experiment." Suddenly, the table soars to the ceiling. Lightning jolts it again and again. The table descends. The body on it moves. "It's alive!" the scientist crows. "It's alive! It's moving! It's alive! It's alive!" A few scenes later, without warning, the monster backs through the lab door. Slowly he turns. In three quick close-ups, each closer than the one before, the audience sees . . . the face.

We have seen the face so many times, in so many parodies, commercials, and Halloween masks, that it is impossible to feel the shock it caused in 1931. Once during the filming of *Frankenstein*, Boris Karloff strolled off the set in full makeup. Turning a corner, he met a studio secretary. She fainted. For the rest of the filming, Karloff was confined to the set between takes, where he sat, in hideous countenance, sipping tea. Now, here he was on-screen—the monster made by "a man of science." On opening nights across the country, audiences cringed. Some walked quickly out of the theater. One mother and daughter ran screaming up the aisle. "Women come out trembling, men exhausted," a critic noted. And of course, horror did Hollywood's bidding, selling tickets in record numbers. *Frankenstein* grossed $12 million. It also watered seeds of suspicion about just what those men of science might be up to.

Frankenstein was not the first caveat that science could create monsters. Science fiction had been imagining mutants for nearly a half century, and there had been a few silent horror films. None, however, had the impact of "the monster" made by Henry Frankenstein. The film spawned an entire genre of "mad scientist films," from *Bride of Frankenstein* to *The Phantom Creeps* to *Attack of the Puppet People*. Taken individually, these films were as silly as their titles, incapable of causing wholesale concern about science. No one who sat through one rushed home to cancel his subscription to *Scientific American.* Yet collectively they presented a side of science rarely seen before. Prior to 1931, science was accorded the utmost respect. Scientists themselves might be oddballs—cold, detached, obsessed with their work—but in the public eye, that work wreaked no havoc. True, science had made war even more monstrous, but it won wars, possibly even shortened them. Science was on our side, and so were scientists. Within living memory, science had made life vastly easier, more efficient, safer. Skepticism of it was limited to cranks and curmudgeons. But with movies like *Frankenstein,* science began showing its other face, causing even true believers to balk at the idea that it was solely a blessing.

Just six weeks before Frankenstein debuted, public perception of science had crossed an equally important threshold. On October 18, 1931, Thomas Edison died. To commemorate him, the government considered shutting off all power for a minute, but decided it was too risky. Edison had invented modern life and become a folk hero in the process. Although he was not strictly a scientist but an electrical engineer, to the public he was the living embodiment of scientific progress. His birthday had been celebrated annually for more than twenty years. His every pronouncement on any topic whatsoever made headlines. He was often hailed as "the greatest living American." With Edison as science's symbol, whatever came out of the lab was synonymous with better living. When he died, science needed a new god. "He was the last and greatest of a long line of experimenters who followed only the dictates of their inner selves," the *New York Times* lamented. "With him the heroic age of invention probably ends. The future belongs to the organized, highly trained physicists and chemists of the corporation research laboratory." Science had passed from the age of Edison to the age of Einstein.

Apart from a broad curiosity and legendary absentmindedness, these two paragons were the yin and yang of science. Edison was the pragmatic inventor, unwilling to consider an invention unless he could foresee its mass market. So long as he was its spokesman, science seemed practical. It was wizardry for the common man—lights, batteries, movies on Saturday night, and phonographs for the rest of the week. Science was made by hard work or, as Edison said, by expending more perspiration than inspiration. Because Edison had very little schooling, it seemed any boy could become a scientist. Science was a lightbulb burning late in a lab. Science was the gathering of wires, switches, and circuitry. Put them together, and Eureka! The scientist made his living by making *things*. Then along came Einstein.

Fourteen years after publishing his theory of relativity, Einstein became famous overnight. During a solar eclipse in 1919, his prediction that light passing a star would be bent by gravity had been proven precisely accurate. Within days, the media were agog about this new universe and the genius who discovered it. As Einstein's fame grew, science took on a different public persona. It was no longer a light in a lab; it was a light going on in a single mind. It was not wires, switches, and circuits you could hold in your hand. It was photons and electrons you couldn't hold no matter how hard you tried. You could talk about splitting the atom, but you couldn't do it at home in your spare time. The cyclotron was scarcely something you could be the first on your block to own, and $E=mc^2$ looked more like a misprint than a blueprint. The very opposite of a self-made inventor, Einstein was a dreamer, a visionary. To be an Edison, you just had to knuckle down. To be an Einstein, you had to be born brilliant.

As Einstein's star rose in public, Edison's flickered and died. The latter's inventions lived on, but the science he stood for seemed like yesterday's magic. It was like those stage tricks that amazed you until you brought a few home in a Mysto set and saw how they were done. When even children could perform magic—turning on a light, changing the batteries, playing the phonograph— it was time for a new act. By 1931 it was easy to think that everything practical had been invented. Hence a scientist no longer made *things;* he made theories. Time was when any Gilbert boy could dream of growing up to be another Edison, but science's new folk hero was well out of reach. Gilbert would try to reach him later, but by then, boyhood was shrinking beyond his grasp.

By coincidence but not by blood, the man who did the most to shrink boyhood was also named Gilbert. Growing up in Chicago between the world wars, Eugene Gilbert might have been one of A. C.'s engineering disciples, but he more closely resembled his namesake in the field of marketing. In the waning months of World War II, Eugene Gilbert got a job in a shoe store. Noting that none of his high school friends knew the store even existed, he made a deal with his boss. Loafers, wing tips, saddle shoes—he could find out exactly what footwear teens wanted, he said. How? By asking them. Marketers were only beginning to survey teens, yet Eugene knew his friends usually lied to adults who asked about their tastes. So he hired teens he nicknamed "Joe Guns" to poll their peers. Then he packaged the data and began peddling it nationwide. His timing was perfect, coinciding with many social trends that were converging to create the modern teenager.

High school enrollment, which had been about 15 percent when the first Erector sets came out, had risen steadily ever since. Eighty percent of teenagers were now in high school, making it a stage on which adolescents dressed up for each other. Prosperity likewise played a part, giving teens more money while keeping their parents steadily employed and out of the way. Coming of age after World War II, boys and girls had more free cash, free time, and free will than any adolescents before them, and they were determined to make the most of their freedom. Once again the nation wrung its hands over a "boy problem," now dubbed "juvenile delinquency." These two words set off a national panic, resulting in the usual responses—congressional hearings, magazine articles, groups of parents getting together. This time, however, Erector sets would not solve the problem. Boys needed more than toys. They needed a host of new products.

Making hundreds of surveys in the next decade, Eugene

Gilbert almost single-handedly created the teenage consumer. He advised the U.S. Army, the Coast Guard, and companies making skin creams, soft drinks, cereals, typewriters, pens, footwear, watches, cars, radios, hi-fis, cameras, shampoo, hair tonic, and on and on. The teen market, Eugene Gilbert told his clients, was "the one market in constant need of ALL products." Advertisers drooled. In new magazines like *Seventeen* and *Hot Rod,* ads began smelling like teen spirit. The pitches to boys became younger, more macho, tinged with power and success. Cokes once enjoyed with Mom and Dad became Cokes on the beach with a girlfriend. Cereals that had been merely "nutritious" now helped an ordinary boy become a basketball star. And the army, whose ads had always peddled patriotism, now asked boys, "What's it worth to feel like a man?" With their tastes bought and sold, boys and girls responded as consumers will. Teen spending rose from $2 billion in 1945 to $10 billion a decade later. And male teenagers began considering themselves a breed apart, much older and tougher than any little boy, and eager to imitate each other, not some aging adult.

A. C. Gilbert had seen boys as customers, but also as young minds in need of nurturing. Eugene Gilbert saw them as shoppers. And shoppers they became. A shopper still has time to build and experiment, of course. Saving his allowance, a shopper might even buy his own Erector set. Yet by the mid-1950s, an entire teenage tasteland had been created, and the boys who had once idolized A. C. Gilbert now succumbed to other temptations. Boys twelve and under remained boys, sometimes even as innocent as A. C. Gilbert imagined them. But older boys no longer dreamed of becoming men; they dreamed of becoming cool. To hit that moving target, they began delving into fields far removed from science and engineering. Girls. Music. Movies. Girls. TV. Girls. And cars.

Back in 1915, when an Oregon boy stole a car just for the fun of driving, he had been part of the boy problem. By 1950, a boy no longer needed to steal to get behind the wheel. If he couldn't afford his own hot rod, someone in the neighborhood could. Painted candy apple red, dressed in chrome, roaring down the street, hot rods brought many a boy racing from his Erector set to his front window. Before long, he was in a neighbor's garage, talking shop. Forget twelve-inch girders. Forget tiny nuts and bolts. Forget all that kids' stuff. Even a boy of ten or eleven, with an older brother as his guide, could be admitted to a Guys' Club that made Gilbert's look like *Howdy Doody*. Among these guys, the talk was not of girders but of glass packs, not of battery power but of horsepower, 100 horsepower under a flame-decaled hood. Cherry. Once hot rods began cruising just after the war, Gilbert's influence on every boy who chafed at being called a boy was over. By 1960, 44 percent of teenage boys owned their own cars. A first driver's license had become a coming-of-age ritual, but it was only one of many.

The grandsons of boys who made crystal sets could now afford transistor radios. Turning them on, they didn't hear Yale professors making speeches. They tuned in Elvis, Buddy Holly, and the entire hit parade peddling romance and rebellion. On the proverbial rainy afternoon, a boy might unpack his Gilbert microscope, but he was just as likely to see science through a different glass, darkly. On TV, he could watch a sci-fi film where atomic radiation made giant insects that had just eaten Chicago and were headed for Detroit. "But professor! You're a scientist! Surely you don't believe this *thing* can't be stopped!" This was the new public image of science—dangerous, destructive, nerdy. And come Christmas or a birthday, an Erector set was often well down a boy's list, almost an afterthought after a record player or a Fender Stratocaster.

Fast cars, rock records, and peer pressure combined to make the postwar adolescent boy a distant cousin of Gilbert's steady customers. The change did not happen with a single movie, nor did it begin with the death of a single inventor. Cultural revolutions, unlike their political counterparts, are in continuous ebb and flow. Throughout the 1950s, there were still plenty of Gilbert boys, and Erector sets continued to sell. Yet the handwriting was on the hardware. From the moment teenage culture took root, Gilbert began to lose constituents. First to leave the fold were the older teens, who also cut their membership in the Boy Scouts by half. Next to slip away were boys slightly younger, who began to imitate their peers instead of some paterfamilias. As teenhood trickled down, boyhood grew shorter every decade, until these days it is not surprising to meet boys (and girls) who seem eight going on fifteen. Gilbert, like many adults overwhelmed by this wave, couldn't begin to surf it. He could only struggle to keep his head above water.

Having been an early broadcaster, Gilbert remained savvy about boy media. After World War II, comic books and TV became the best channels for reaching boys, and Gilbert tried both. Though his media were modern, his message seemed ancient. As Christmas approached in 1948, Gilbert sponsored *Roar of the Rails,* a fifteen-minute drama in which kindly old Grandpa James told tales of his railroading days. Grandpa's adventures were then acted out on elaborate American Flyer layouts. The show, which returned for Christmas the following year, also featured Gilbert's first TV commercials, done live in the studio. The following year, Gilbert promoted his trains on *The American Flyer Boys' Railroad Club.* Filmed at the Gilbert Hall of Science, the "club" featured boys goshing and gollying over huge train layouts while a guest from a real railroad spoke of his job. Only six of the shows were made, however. Watching model trains run on TV wasn't quite the same as owning one.

Gilbert comic books seemed equally dated. For a moment, imagine—or remember—what it was like to be a boy in the 1950s. You have ten minutes to kill before school. You have a stack of comics. Which do you reach for? *Superman? Batman? The Green Hornet?* Or the one in which Aristotle, disguised as "Mr. Science," takes a boy named Bud on a tour of Lavoisier's lab? "Science is more interesting than you think, young man!"

Mr. Science says in Gilbert's comic. "Maybe so, Mister," Bud replies. "But where's the adventure in it?" Many boys, asking the same, reached for a comic whose hero who didn't sound like their chemistry teacher.

Nearly two decades after Edison's passing led to the age of Einstein, Gilbert tried to blend the former's pragmatism with the latter's theories. The result was the Gilbert U-238 Atomic Energy Lab, released in 1950. The lab brought the tools of Oak Ridge and Los Alamos—those places parents had been hearing so much about lately—right into their living room. Each Atomic Energy Lab included:

1. a battery-powered Geiger counter;
2. an electroscope for detecting alpha particles in an ionization chamber;
3. a Gilbert Cloud Chamber to detect the path of charged subatomic particles;
4. a spinthariscope that "shows you actual Atomic disintegration of radioactive material!";
5. several "nuclear spheres";
6. four glass jars containing radioactive autunite, torbernite, uraninite, and carnotite mined from the "Colorado plateau region";
7. a sixty-page manual;
8. a copy of *Dagwood Splits the Atom*, in which the hapless *Blondie* comics hero is shrunk to molecular size to split an atom and explain the process. ("I give up! I can't put a dent in that nucleus any more than I can loosen up my boss for a raise.")

All this atomic gear came in a wooden box and sold for $50. Once the kit was on toy store shelves, you no longer had to be a rocket scientist to play with the building blocks of the atomic age. In fact, the less a boy knew, the more comfortable he would feel bringing atomic radiation into his own bedroom. As with other Gilbert science kits, college professors consulted on the manual.

The booklet assumed its user, shown with Brylcreemed hair, to be a budding Einstein. Familiar with algebra, he was able to assemble a Cloud Chamber and could be trusted to handle small hunks of radioactive particles. The manual featured a lengthy explanation of the Inverse Square Law governing radioactivity's strength at varying distances. It also explained the properties of alpha, beta, and gamma rays and how to detect them. But being a Gilbert book, the U-238 Atomic Energy Manual knew that boys just wanted to have fun. While it never promised to make a mushroom cloud appear, the booklet encouraged boys to play "hide and seek with the gamma ray source." "The person who is selected to find the gamma ray source is given the Geiger counter and told to wait outside the room while the others hide the source. Then after the source has been hidden, the outsider is invited in and told to look for it." When the Geiger counter began to click about 200 times per minute, the seeker was getting warm, warmer, warm-errrr! Once he found the ore, someone else could be "it." "Prizes can be awarded to the person who finds it in the shortest time."

Radioactivity could be dangerous, the manual warned, yet not all that dangerous. "There has been so much misinformation about radioactivity that we pause here to reassure you and your parents that the radioactive sources supplied to you are not dangerous in any way." Still, users should not take ore samples out of their jars, "for they tend to flake and crumble and you would run the risk of having radioactive ore spread out in your laboratory. This will raise the level of the background count." The atom is your friend, the manual noted. Someday radiation would propel submarines, attack cancer, and grow better food. In the meantime, just ignore those nasty rumors of radioactive hazard. "These hazards have been greatly exaggerated by the modern world. People often fear something they know very little about. The only way to make them forget these fears is to give them the facts of radioactive hazards. Throughout the manual you will find these facts will show you that you can deal with radioactivity if you can recognize it." And if, Geiger counter in hand, a boy recognized radioactivity anywhere outside his lab, he might win $10,000. "That's what the United States government will pay to anyone who discovers deposits of Uranium Ore!"

Gilbert was not alone in soft-selling atomic energy during the infancy of the nuclear arms race. Barely a day after the bombing of Hiroshima, pop culture began soothing fears. Songs such as "Atom Bomb Baby" and "Jesus Hits Like an Atom Bomb" topped country charts. Bars sold atomic cocktails. For 15 cents and a box top, General Mills offered an Atomic Bomb Ring showing "genuine atoms split to smithereens." Newsreels, magazine articles, and the famous civil defense mascot, Bert the Turtle, all told people that the atomic age held no cause for panic. Compared to these, Gilbert's U-238 Atomic Energy Lab was sane and reasoned. His manual made no idle promises of atomic cars, atomic weather control, or atomic energy vitamin tablets. The lab was scientific and informative. Perhaps that's why it didn't sell.

Columbia University bought five of Gilbert's atomic kits for its nuclear physics laboratory. Thousands more sat on toy shelves. In the atomic age, science's cutting edge was not where parents wanted their children to play. More than either Einstein or Frankenstein, "the bomb" abruptly ended the public's love affair with science. Yes, science could make your kitchen more convenient, but it could also level a city. You could trust Edison, but Einstein and his ilk might destroy all life on earth. A boy could dream of being a nuclear physicist, but did that mean he had to bring isotopes into the house? Who knew where those isotopes had been?

Gilbert's Atomic Energy Lab sold fewer than 5,000 units. It was discontinued in 1952. As when he released his wide-ranging science kits, Gilbert had misjudged the toy market. But this time, his problem ran deeper than price and sales. The man who had built his career on boys, repackaging his own boyhood and boasting of being "just a big boy myself" was oblivious to the ways boys were changing. Erector was now older than Gilbert was when he invented it. The boys who had played with the first sets were grown men, eager to buy Erector for their sons and grandsons, but a growing number of those boys were too busy to play with them. And approaching seventy, the king of Connecticut, accustomed to winning ever since he first built an athletic club in his barn, was left to face a foe no one has ever defeated.

> When I was just a wee little lad full of health and joy
> My father homeward came one night and gave to me a toy.
> A wonder to behold, it was, with many colors bright
> And the moment I laid eyes on it, it became my heart's delight.
>
> It went "zip" when it moved and "bop" when it stopped
> And "whirr" when it stood still.
> I never knew just what it was
> And I guess I never will.
>
> —TOM PAXTON, "THE MARVELOUS TOY"

10

The Joy Problem

Running on time for a change, Amtrak's Night Owl crept out of New Haven just before dawn on January 9, 1978. Most passengers were asleep as the train inched past the high-voltage towers lining the northbound tracks. The Night Owl was due into Boston at 7:30 A.M., but just a few miles from the station, the train's spotlight fell on something in its path. The engineer braked to a complete stop. Then, to the dismay of awakened passengers, the train backed into the New Haven station. There it waited for Amtrak crews to clear pieces of a bygone era from the tracks.

Gale winds and battering rain had raged all night along the eastern seaboard. No one was hurt and no buildings were damaged, yet sometime during the night, the storm had blown down the radio tower that had stood atop Erector Square since 1921. Like a poorly assembled Erector model, the 125-foot tower crashed onto the tracks below. It took workmen two hours to clear one track, letting the Night Owl pass. It took them several more to cut the tower to pieces with welding torches and cart it to a junkyard. Locals lamented the passing of a landmark, but the tower's fall was only slightly more abrupt than the crash of the A. C. Gilbert Company.

Throughout the late 1950s, with Al Gilbert Jr. at its helm, the company had continued as one of America's best-known toy firms. Annual sales regularly topped $20 million. Nearly half that revenue came from American Flyer, whose line featured boxcars that unloaded hay, steers that climbed ramps into cattle cars, and various bells and whistles. Thanks to 55 million baby boomers, the largest cohort of kids in the nation's history, the company stayed in the black. Yet the rise of home air-conditioning had ruined its Polar Cub fan business. Other Gilbert appliances had also been scrapped, and the company turned a profit only by imposing drastic cost-cutting measures—using lighter-gauge steel and flimsy plastic motors—that cheapened Erector.

Striving to keep boys in tune with contemporary science, Al Gilbert engineered new sets. The Erector Rocket Launcher set enabled a boy to build a ramp and launch his plastic rocket across the room. The Erector Space Age set built missiles, rockets, and planes. Aside from these, however, Erector was a tired old toy. Like a Detroit auto engineer, Al's father had made annual cosmetic changes in his sets, but most of the models had not been updated since 1924. Manuals still featured the Bundle Truck, the Gravel Screen, and a horse-drawn Farm Wagon. Yet nowhere could you find a boy or a girl who knew what a bundle truck or gravel screen might be, and horse-drawn farm wagons could only be seen on *Wagon Train* and other TV Westerns. Boomers fondly remember the 1950s Erector, including the Giant Walking Robot set and cheaper sets that came in tubes, milk cartons, and cardboard boxes. They had no inkling, however, of Erector's former "unsurpassed glory," and Gilbert wasn't around to tell them.

"What I'll probably do is compromise and become chairman of the board," Gilbert had predicted upon retiring at the age of seventy. "I'm afraid I'd feel lost if I dropped out of this race. I'm willing to let Al worry about new cost accounting systems, time studies, and finances, and run the business, but I'm going to have plenty to do and say about engineering, new inventions, and products ... for many years to come." Gilbert's son was typically diplomatic about the transition. "Dad gets frustrated because he still can't run the whole show, but he never stops trying," Al said. Yet only a few years after he stepped down, the elder Gilbert's restless energy began to flag. Aging visibly, he seemed a skeleton inside his flannel shirts. His perpetual scowl turned into a weak, almost apologetic smile, and he compared himself to "an athlete gone stale." He rarely went to the office, offered only sporadic advice to his son, and never returned to his Northwest hunting grounds. When the entire Gilbert clan gathered for dinner, he said less and less. Though Mary doted on her grandchildren, they still found their grandfather aloof. "All of us kept begging for attention from him," said grandson Sev Marsted, "but the business was his life really. After a while, you didn't expect attention. You knew you couldn't sit in his chair and whenever he entered the room behavior took on a different tone. He was never rude or cruel to us, just distant."

Gilbert had accomplished as much as any boy might dream of. From the playing fields of Idaho to the Olympics in London, from a two-room toy workshop to a huge toy factory, from the days when boys were a problem to the days when they were his disciples, he had won every race and cleared every bar. With his company turned over to his son, there was little left for the patriarch to do but roam his estate. The grounds were considerably smaller, owing to Gilbert's own development of homes along their perimeter. The modern sprawl of highways, housing, and shopping centers had begun to encroach on his own private Paradise, yet it still had room for an old man in a tattered jacket, walking with his favorite dog through the Connecticut woods.

Resting now beside the pond that reflects his log cabin lodge, Gilbert thinks back over his seventy-some years. He remembers a boys' fire department that answered calls from a barn and a vaudeville magician who called "that fine looking boy on the aisle" to come up onstage and help him with a few tricks. He recalls the afternoon in 1901 when he did forty chin-ups, then dropped to the floor. He envisions a wiry lad in a track uniform with a big Y on it, sprinting down a runway, bamboo pole poised to send him flying. He waxes nostalgic about meeting Teddy Roosevelt and remembers a young businessman full of pep leaping around a hotel room to show off his new toy. Each event was "the biggest day of my life," he thinks. Each was "the most exciting thing that ever happened to me." But each was so long ago.

In January 1961, a week before the new president announced that "the torch has been passed to a new generation of Americans," Gilbert was hospitalized following a heart attack. After making some progress, he suffered a second heart attack on January 24. The following day, newspapers across the nation paid tribute to the man who had "brightened the lives of millions of small boys and their fathers." A front-page obituary in the *New York Times* praised Gilbert as a blend of "Frank Merriwell, Theodore Roosevelt, Peter Pan, and Horatio Alger heroes." Like an Alger protagonist, the *Times* noted, Gilbert had "developed a $20,000,000-a-year business out of a shoestring start as an amateur magician." The obit repeated the story of the serendipitous train ride during which Gilbert conceived Erector. It charted the rocket rise of the toy and even recycled the shopworn myth that its inventor had been "a frail child." Touting his string of successes in pole vaulting, business, and later in hunting, the *Times* observed, "Finally, and through it all, Mr. Gilbert never really left boyhood behind him." As an epitaph, the *Times* quoted Gilbert's telltale credo: "Everything in life is a game but the important thing is to win." Gilbert, the obit concluded, was survived by his wife, three children, and ten grandchildren.

Toy makers, even when they stamp their names on their playthings, usually live in anonymity, earning publicity only in trade journals or a paper's business section. Yet Gilbert, having spoken as a second father to America's boys, earned their fond remembrance. Newspapers and magazines across the country echoed the *Times*'s praise. Many adults who were by then driving cars they couldn't repair themselves and watching TVs far more complex than any crystal radio saw in Gilbert's death the passing of a simpler era built of nuts and bolts. All his life Gilbert had stood for staunch Victorian values—education, fairness, and the virtues of remaining wide-awake. Yet upon his death, the press remembered him as perhaps the last man lucky enough to play for a living. *Newsweek* headlined his obit "Happiest Millionaire," ignoring Gilbert's scowl in the accompanying photo of him beside an Erector Ferris Wheel. The same photo ran with *Time*'s obit, headlined "Just a Boy." "For two generations of American boys, the name of A. C. Gilbert has evoked the magic of discovery and invention," *Time* noted. After sharing with readers the same rags-to-riches story, the magazine lamented Gilbert's passing while "still young at seventy-six."

In the end it mattered little that Gilbert was far less boyish than he or the press proclaimed. If a boy, however small, lives on in every man, then that boy wants to believe in a bigger lad who never had to knuckle down and grow up. And so the truth about Gilbert never made it into the obituaries. Gilbert was far from the happiest millionaire, nor was he "just a boy." His own claims of insouciance to the contrary, he was a businessman who, unlike his peers, had the luxury of an idyllic boyhood on which to base his business. With no sense of irony, he toiled like a workaholic to promote such a childhood as the birthright of every American boy. Rarely relaxing, always inquiring about what boys might like to play with next, he sacrificed his own sense of play in order to mass-market a playful spirit of discovery.

Gilbert was not the first adult to devote his life to toys, but he was the first to take toys and their influence seriously. As such, he was the father of the educational toy business. Never in it for the money, he sincerely believed in the power of a toy to open a mind and make a difference in the life of any child. Decades before progressive schoolteachers made a mantra of the phrase "hands on," the conservative, straitlaced Gilbert knew that children learn primarily by playing. He explained his philosophy before the House Ways and Means Committee in 1921. "At the same time that we try to teach the boy something," he said, "we attempt to keep fun in front of him, so that he does not really discover that he is being taught anything." Gilbert went on to ask the committee for a 60 percent tariff to keep German toy imports at bay after World War I. Impressed by his testimony and, of course, the toys he passed around, Congress gave him 70 percent, and the American toy industry never looked back.

But Gilbert's passing meant more than the end of the nuts-and-bolts era. It also marked the end of toys as a gentleman's business. The billions that boomers poured into the toy trade took the industry beyond the control of individual families and into the realm of corporate boards, stockholders, and consultants. Less than a decade earlier, a conscientious toy maker could still take things into his own hands as Gilbert did one Christmas Eve in the early 1950s. During dinner at Maraldene, he received a call from a father in New Orleans. The man had ordered an American Flyer set for his son, but the dealer had not yet received it. The father didn't have to tell Gilbert how his son would feel on Christmas morning. Gilbert thanked the man, then quickly called a member of his sales department. He got the name of the dealer in New Orleans and his regional supplier. He called them both, making sure the train set got to the store and into the man's hands that evening. Then he sent the man a check to cover the cost of his long-distance call. That, as much as any change in toys, was what passed with Gilbert. The coming years would show how much had been lost.

More than any other toy maker in history, Gilbert made the modern toy business. He waged the first nationwide toy campaign, proving that toys could be more than mere trinkets tossed to children each Christmas. Realizing that toys, like any other business, deserved their own trade organization, he founded the Toy Manufacturers of America. He saved one Christmas and lobbied in Washington, D.C., to make many more bountiful. His personal pitches to parents and their sons could be found in living rooms wherever magazines sat on coffee tables. In more than forty years on the job, Gilbert had taken the toy industry from its infancy to its adolescence. Now it remained for others to send the trade spinning into adulthood.

✦

With his father gone, Al Gilbert tried to drag the company into the space age. He added a Cape Canaveral Erector along with kits teaching electrical engineering and fluid dynamics. A slot car set sold well, yet overall sales slipped, inheritance taxes were stiff, and the Gilbert family was left holding more property than it could afford. Less than a year after his father's death, Al had had enough. As if auctioning the crown, he sold all the family stock, giving a controlling interest in the company to a Beverly Hills businessman. Jack Wrather's other holdings included the Disneyland Hotel in Anaheim, the TV shows *Lassie* and *The Lone Ranger*, and Muzak, the company that piped canned music into offices and elevators. Wrather would eventually become one of Ronald Reagan's "kitchen cabinet," the group of wealthy businessmen who encouraged Reagan to run for governor of California and then backed him all the way to the White House. But first this son of a Texas oil tycoon had to run Gilbert's company into the ground. He had plenty of help.

As profits dried up and coworkers were laid off, some blamed Al Jr., who remained as president. Others pointed the finger at Jack Wrather and the executives he hired, who just didn't understand toys. But the list of suspects should also include the Gilbert toys themselves. The company that once made the world's greatest toy began turning out "flimsy flamsy gimcracks." Both Erector and American Flyer were dumbed down as if "wide-awake" boys had been lulled into a stupor. Ride 'em Erector boasted that it made a jeep, a scooter, and a racer big enough for a boy to ride on. Three models! They might as well

have announced, "Hello Boys! Make Fewer Toys!" American
Flyer's "All Aboard" set came in prefab panels, enabling boys to
quickly snap together pieces containing track, trees, lakes,
bridges, and buildings. Gosh, Dad, this isn't any fun at all! Other
toys were equally unfriendly. Gilbert's Wing Thing was a "replica
of the wing astronauts will use in returning from space." It's a
good thing the astronauts didn't use it, because it didn't fly. My
Mixer and Scrubble Bubble offered girls more girlish toys. Tun-
ing in pop culture, the company saddled Gilbert's good name
with "My Favorite Martian" Magic Tricks, games based on the
TV shows *Honey West* and *The Man from U.N.C.L.E.,* and a
James Bond 007 Road Race set. James Bond dealt Gilbert the
coup de grâce. Sears ordered $6 million worth of the sets one
Christmas. Inventory problems kept the factory from filling the
order, and half the sets sent out had defects and had to be returned.

But if Gilbert toys were no longer the brightest bulbs under
the tree, they were only following a nationwide trend. The
changes Gilbert had brought to toy marketing—widespread advertising and a personal touch—had been plugged into television.
Soon Gilbert's other innovation—quality—was lost in the waste-
land. As boomers made toys big business, other family toy companies were taken over by corporations. CBS bought Ideal Toys.
General Mills purchased Lionel Trains. Quaker Oats bought
Fisher-Price. Pitching their products on Saturday morning car-
toons, these huge companies did not speak to children like some
doting father. No one's name was signed at the bottom of ads, but
neither kids nor their parents seemed to care. To get a child's attention, all TV had to do was shout, be cute, or pump up the action. "Anything advertised on television sells," one buyer told
the toy trade journal *Playthings.* And so anything sold. An enter-
prising child could still get an Erector set, but bolting together
girders couldn't compete with the instant fun of Frisbees, Silly
Putty, Crashmobiles, Barbie, GI Joe, Mister Machine, Robot
Commando, and a roomful of toys licensed to kiddie shows.

In the midst of this nonstop fun, a staid old toy company, hierarchical in its management and hidebound in tradition, didn't stand a chance. As the A. C. Gilbert Company went down, Al desperately tried to save his father's empire. He boosted TV advertising and hired one of the nation's top toy designers. Sales continued to slide. Then in June 1964, Gilbert coworkers were shocked to learn that their president had been hospitalized. A week later, leaving behind a wife, four children, and a life dutifully led in his father's shadow, Al Gilbert died of a brain tumor. He was forty-four.

Under new management, the company did better the following year, but by 1967 it had lost $20 million since its founder's death. Early that year, the A. C. Gilbert Company laid off its final coworkers. Then the company closed the lid, put its sets away, and ended fifty-eight years in the toy business. Over the next decade, the rest of Gilbert's kingdom was liquidated. His empty factory was sold to a developer who struggled to attract business before discovering that artists like to rent studios in gloomy old factories. Paradise was subdivided into single-family houses, with its final pristine acreage becoming the Laurel View Country Club. Gilbert's hunting lodge fell to a wrecker's ball. His big-game trophies were donated to Yale's Peabody Museum of Natural History, which kept a few but auctioned the rest at Christie's in New York. The biggest bear went for $4,000. American Flyer was sold to Lionel shortly after the Gilbert Company folded. And Erector?

Since the 1920s, the trademarked name has been generic for any construction toy. Even today, journalists describe new bridges and towers as looking like giant Erector sets. As Erector struggled on through the 1970s and '80s, however, the sets themselves got smaller, less intricate, and less interesting. Gone were most of Gilbert's own innovations—the patented lip that interlocked and strengthened girders, the motors, the wide range of parts and models. The familiar trademark bounced from company to company. It changed hands three times in the last decade alone as sales dropped to less than $1 million. Erector is currently a trademark of Meccano SN of France. Meccano is revving up Erector, turning out sets that promise power and action. The sets are distributed in America by Brio, the toy train maker. Some of today's Erector sets include a handful of models that offer specialized plastic parts kids can assemble into big-wheeled vehicles, including tractors, fire trucks, and heavy equipment. Those for ages four to eight come with small plastic men, suggesting that the fun is in the playing more than in the putting-together. The bigger sets for kids eight to thirteen, however, approach Erector's old glory. They range from small two-model kits to hefty sets with 600 metal parts that make fifty different models. A new Special Edition Train Set harks back to Gilbert's Hudson Locomotive; it can be used to build a smaller, battery-powered version. And Erector's Crazy Inventors series lets kids from "ages 8–88" build flying bats, steamboats, even a zeppelin, just like their grandfathers did. Yet no matter how glorious the new Erector sets become, they face competition much tougher than Gilbert ever knew, in a toy industry whose annual sales now top $34 billion.

⚒

Taxis are triple-parked along Eleventh Avenue on a brisk, breezy February morning in midtown Manhattan. Causing backups along the thoroughfare overlooking the Hudson River, the taxis take their time letting passengers exit. Emerging from the cabs are dozens of straight-faced, purposeful men in suits and women in blazers. Today they will attend the American International Toy Fair, still hosted each February by the trade group Gilbert founded, in 2001 renamed the Toy Industry Association. The Toy Fair is far removed from the "bedroom industry" fair where Gilbert first showed Erector in his hotel room in 1913. Now the Toy Fair, like huge computer and auto trade shows, is held in the towering steel-and-glass halls of the Jacob K. Javits Center. As in Gilbert's day, the fair is a coming-out party for the hottest toys of the coming Christmas. More than 1,700 exhibitors from ninety-nine countries are on hand to display their "product." Seminars explore such topics as "The Changing Face of Children: Niche Marketing in a Diverse Market Place," "High-Tech Toys and Girls," and "Toy Industry Licensing: Beyond Schmooze! How Deals Are Done." For four days, 40,000 people talk toys, do deals, and try to turn fun into a going concern.

At first glance, the Toy Fair seems like an enormous playroom. All the familiar classics from the history of toys are here— hundreds of different dolls, rocking horses, toy guns, games of every stripe, bikes, trikes, planes, boats, and trains, Lincoln Logs and teddy bears, even those old favorite pranks—snapping gum and joy buzzers. Each plaything is prominently displayed in a brightly colored booth bustling with freshly scrubbed sales staff looking anxious, bored, or eager. It seems as if toy makers, merchants, and consultants, surrounded by all these playthings, should be having fun, yet the Toy Fair is Serious Business. In an industry where billions depend on secrecy and surprise, commerce long ago trumped any lingering sense of play. Gilbert didn't smile much either, another legacy he left to his successors. But at least the toys are enjoying themselves. On small TVs, huge video screens, and display counters, toys leap and twirl, coo and cuddle. If computerized, they just stand up and introduce themselves. One magnetic top even levitates, spinning a few inches in the air. Thousands of toys. Row after row. Aisle after aisle. It's enough to make a child drool, if only children were allowed in this adults-only fair.

As toys change and toy companies come and go, each fair has a different flavor. But one perennial question hangs over the crowd: What will be the Tickle Me Elmo of the coming Christmas? Which toy will become so hot it will fly off the shelves, make parents pay scalper's prices, delight children on Christmas, and lie abandoned in closets by the following summer?

What will it be this year? Remote-control robotic insects that
bump, bash, and pinch each other? A home karaoke machine for
the lounge lizard lurking in your playroom? Or one of the gazil-
lion trinkets—nearly half of all toys now sold—tied to a hit
movie, cartoon show, or pop diva with a bare midriff? At recent
fairs, attention has focused on "smart toys," part toy, part computer, and mostly gadget. While overall toy sales dropped in 2000
and rose less than 2 percent the following year, sales of smart toys
have skyrocketed. Throughout the fair, any toy that has a computer chip and a voice of its own is considered prime property. In
the fair's TechnoPlay section, robotic dogs walk, speak, and
scratch themselves on voice command. Dolls talk back to girls,
complaining if they are forced to wear pajamas all day. A teddy
bear sings, tells stories, and can be plugged into a computer key-
board to download everything he knows. Push a button, and robotic fish swim. Talking dump trucks say, "We mean business,
right, buddy?" There are no other words for these techno-toys
but . . . *why bother?*

If toys had IQs, smart toys might be geniuses. But you don't
have to be what Louis Marx derided as "hermetically sealed parents who wash their children 1,000 times a day" to ask whether
smart toys make smart children. Some of the best computerized
toys introduce kids to reading and math, talking them through
stories and simple problems, but most are just chatty. As toys get
smarter, what happens to the dumb toys that just sit there, begging for a child's imagination? There are still many such toys, yet
they're too modest to speak for themselves. Elsewhere at the Toy
Fair, construction kits such as K'nex, Zoob, and a clever new one
called KnuckleStrutz let kids build with interconnecting plastic
doohickeys. The results may not mirror any construction you're
likely to see on the street, but each requires a child to think and
explore. Perhaps that's why they aren't likely to be this year's
hottest toys. Construction toys now account for just 3 percent of
the American toy market. And while no one would deny that
toys are safer than ever—today's chemistry sets offer warning la-

bels on every chemical, including acetic acid, aka vinegar—are they really smarter?

Once this fair full of toys makes it to market, parents who know where to look will find some of them far more enriching than those of Gilbert's day. Stores specializing in educational toys feature kits about ancient Egypt and the Middle Ages, games based on the solar system and the stock market, and labs that help kids explore nature, build motors, and do behavioral experiments with their cats or dogs. Gilbert would have been heartened by such toys—until he saw the bottom line. In 2001, total sales of these "learning/exploration" toys was $464 million, a mere pittance compared with the top-selling category—video games. Led by Nintendo, Sega, PlayStation2, and Microsoft's Xbox, these games raked in $9.4 billion in 2001, 43 percent more than the previous year and triple the total of the next largest category. This steamroller in the toy trade concerns parents, professors, and other adults who take toys seriously.

Writing in *American Scientist*, Henry Petroski, author of several popular books on engineering and design, laments computerized play and the demise of the "toys that built engineers." "Whereas the budding engineer once had to wrestle with the nuts and bolts of Erector sets, always planning ahead to be sure the fingers could reach behind the parts of the construction crane, delivery truck or bridge being assembled, today's youngsters command armies of destruction workers without ever having to construct any one of them. Today's engineering students may have played with Legos, but to the Erector set veteran Legos seem more like puzzles than construction toys. As a rule, today's future engineers play electronic games rather than design them. One begins to wonder what these children of cyberspace will do when they encounter the real world of engineering, which does not come with prepackaged software or with everything preprogrammed."

But while it's easy to blame toy manufacturers—and fun, too!—there's no problem with toys that couldn't be solved by a little parental discretion. Children today want exactly what Gillie wanted—magic. Sensory surprises evoke the startle reflex, waking children from their ambient boredom. Something disappears—eyes widen. Something reappears—eyebrows go up. Something speaks or moves on its own power—hands reach for it, eager to make the magic happen again. In the 1890s Gillie made his own magic, then carved a career out of helping boys make their own. In too many modern playrooms, technology makes things appear, disappear, speak, and move. There is no effort or creativity, no demand for practice or mastery. All the hard work is done by adults, who often spend years programming their techno-toys. Gilbert's toys encouraged boys to perform for parents and friends. Today, *toys* are the performers, making children the audience. And that, say psychologists and many parents, is the problem.

Children are the best salesmen on earth, charming, well informed, and persistent. Yet parents do not have to buy what children are selling. No parent is forced to spring for toys that offer children little more than instant gratification. If toys are talking more now—and you can't get some toys to shut up—parents can talk back. They can ask questions about toys. According to Stevanne Auerbach, Ph.D., the toy consultant who bills herself as "Dr. Toy," before buying a toy, parents should ask:

1. Is the toy age-appropriate?
2. Is the toy well designed and safe?
3. Is the toy something the child will enjoy using for a long time?
4. Does the toy stimulate creativity?
5. Will it teach—expanding positive self-esteem, values, understanding, and cultural awareness, eye-hand coordination, fine and large motor skills, computer or communication skills, or understanding of the environment, the community, the world?
6. Will the toy frustrate or challenge the child?
7. Will the toy help to nurture childhood?
8. Can the child use the toy alone?

9. Is there any violence, sexism, or negative aspect to the product?
10. Is the toy fun?

"A child should be able to play with a toy at his own pace and develop it with his own imagination," says Dr. Toy, who admits to having played with her cousin's Erector set and "feeling very jealous that he got to have something so special and so shiny"; Erector "was magical in that you could create whatever you wanted, and it looked so real." Dr. Toy—the title stems from her doctorate in child development—thinks today's children would play with Erector sets, even those from Gilbert's era, if given a chance. "If you just turn off the TV and give a child something fascinating to work on, the child will jump at it and love it," she said. "Part of the problem is that we don't give them the chance."

The problem with too many contemporary toys is their removal from the world as we find it. Video games, computer games, Game Boys—all exist in a netherworld of bits and bytes. Millions of children spend hours with these toys. Who can blame them? The graphics are awesome, the action is nonstop, and playing with them is just like living, sort of. Yet when these digital worlds are turned off, their lessons live on solely in the mind. Kids do not pass digital buildings on their way to school. They do not wave to Pokémon characters. They do not see superheroes or gladiators on the street. No skateboard can do on concrete what you can make it do onscreen. Children under ten have always thrived on such fantasy, yet video games, with their deep labyrinths of mystery, extend the unreality well into adolescence. And so the longer children are plugged into these toys, the more they live in two realms—the toy world, in which they are masters controlling every move, and that other world, dull and disenchanting, where they must live as powerless peasants. No link, girder, or model connects the two. No wonder so many teens feel unwelcome as they are shoved toward an adulthood from which their amusements have utterly estranged them.

When he changed the way boys and toys were made, A. C. Gilbert didn't need digital magic. He merely bridged the playroom with the world beyond it. Fire trucks, dolls, and trains already modeled society, yet only Gilbert recruited boys to help him with his bridge. In doing so, he smoothed the transition from childhood to adulthood, which is never easy without guidance. Nearly a century later, in an age that prides itself on complexity, even in its toys, this seems like a simple idea, too simple to work. But ask the man who built the bridge. "I guess my life hasn't been anything to set the world on fire," Gilbert once noted, "but it's been interesting, and I know this: I've had more fun than the average boy. What with the trains and everything else, I've built an empire. True, it's a toy empire, but isn't this a wonderful thing I've done—for the kids, I mean?" Down through the years, millions of kids nod their heads in agreement.

> *The youth gets together his materials to build*
> *a bridge to the moon, or, perchance, a palace or*
> *temple on the earth, and, at length, the middle-aged*
> *man concludes to build a woodshed with them.*
> —HENRY DAVID THOREAU

Epilogue

When it was finished in 1889, the Eiffel Tower drew that haughty, indignant wrath for which Parisians are justly famous. Petitions demanded it be taken down. Artists and writers mocked it as "a metallic carcass" and "a factory chimney." By 1909, having served its purpose in celebrating the centennial of the French Revolution, the tower was scheduled for demolition. But then someone discovered it made an excellent radio antenna. Soon, to the embarrassment of locals, it became the symbol of Paris. Even today, Parisians are indifferent toward their world-famous landmark. Few would be caught gawking up at it like some *touriste.* Yet the French might feel better about their own Eiffel Tower if they saw mine.

Building an Erector Eiffel Tower was easier than I had imagined. I simply rattled through my set for every curved girder in stock. I found a dozen. Four slow, gentle curves seemed right for the legs. Four more would form the elegant arches beneath the main platform. The final four would sweep skyward. From there, it was just a question of finding the right brackets to bolt the curves together, then adding straight girders to complete the tower's upper reaches. I had to bend some steel to give the structure the proper elegance, twisting the legs to make them flare out. The twisted girders would never be the same again, but neither was I once I'd been to Paris. Two hours of bolting, tightening, and *voilà!*

No sooner was it built than my Eiffel Tower came out of the attic to take a prominent place on our dining room table. Light and small—about eighteen inches high—it became a conversation piece at dinner. Much of the conversation focused on the theme *What in the world is happening to your father?*

What was happening to me? Nothing more than the reclamation of a botched Erector childhood, thank you. Nothing less than proving myself no longer Erector-impaired. By making two Gilbert models and designing my own, I had redeemed the hapless eight-year-old who couldn't build his way out of boredom. True, my Eiffel Tower wasn't postcard-perfect. The upper platform was bright red, crowned by a brass gear. Single-girder construction made the tower seem almost two-dimensional when viewed from the side. And the whole thing tilted a little, as if it were the Leaning Tower of Paris. All in all, it resembled Eiffel's masterpiece about as much as a bag of French fries tastes like haute cuisine. But I could put my Erector set away knowing I, too, was a Gilbert boy, part of the long legacy.

The legacy begot by 30 million Erector sets continues today, yet it is a mixed one. America remains a nation of builders, but we have grown ambivalent about our talent. We can still build things that inspire awe—palatial domed stadiums, crystalline skyscrapers, the Internet. Yet building often seems like our national obsession. Driven not just by antlike instinct but also by the profit motive, we scar our gorgeous landscape with malls, offices, freeways, gas stations, and other sprawl, much of it no more stylish than if it had been built from Erector sets. Since Gilbert's passing, this urge has only accelerated, spreading concrete and girders from sea to shining sea. Gilbert boys seem to have done their jobs too well. Their engineering feats, once heroic, now seem routine, less worthy of our attention than the work of athletes, actors, and musicians.

Yet there was a time when building seemed as natural and important as a sand castle seems to a child on a beach, bucket and shovel in hand. And science was a nurturing parent known not just to nerds. Early in Gilbert's era, any kid could name a living scientist—Edison, of course, but also Luther Burbank, Guglielmo Marconi, Charles P. Steinmetz, and the Curies. Gilbert boys who had been reading *Erector Tips* could also name a civil engineer or two. Works in progress, from the smallest crystal radio to the tallest skyscraper, were the stuff of dreams, and serious play that mimicked adult work seemed the best kind. This play was Gilbert's legacy. Nearly ninety years after the first Erector set, however, Gilbert's influence in the world beyond the playroom is difficult to pin down. No one knows how many mechanics, machinists, construction foremen, draftsmen, electricians, scientists, inventors, and engineers of all stripes got their start from an ad that announced "Hello Boys—Make Lots of Toys!" But at least three generations of boys (and an assortment of girls) learned the basics of construction by piecing together little Boom Derricks and Revolving Cranes. Perhaps only a fraction of them went on to build things for a living, but most came to appreciate a well-made work of engineering. And they kept busy by making things instead of breaking things.

"Every Boy Has Two Sides," an early Gilbert ad proclaimed. Beneath drawings of boys building Erector and boys running from a store window shattered by a brick, the ad explained Gilbert's bipolar theory of boyhood: "A boy is likely to be destructive and engage in mischievous pranks simply because he hasn't anything else to do. Give him something to do which is not only constructive and useful but also has the essential element of fun—then you'll see how easy it is to suppress his destructive side and develop his constructive side. That was my aim in inventing Erector." Boys have never been this black and white; many, including Gilbert's own son, had instincts he never acknowledged. Yet Erector, far better than any toy of its time, encouraged the hand that builds while subduing the hand that grips the brick.

But Erector has a more lasting legacy. Small girders cannot

build full-scale machines, but some adults found them ideal for making prototypes that grew into devices we still use today.

During the Great Depression, William Sewell's favorite toy was his Erector set. Even when he enrolled in Yale Medical School, he had a passion for building. By 1949, the med school had changed dramatically since Gilbert's graduation. No one could study just four years as an undergrad, then hang out a shingle. Medicine required graduate work, an internship, and a thesis. Sewell's thesis project was to build the first functional artificial heart. He built it with his trusty Erector set.

Heart surgery was still in its stone age. Doctors had learned to tie off veins and arteries while making minor repairs to a beating heart, yet they knew major surgery would be impossible until a patient's blood could be kept flowing with an artificial pump while surgeons operated on a stopped heart. But could a machine duplicate the human heart? Sewell was among the first to try making one. His device was designed to replace only the heart's right half. It would receive oxygen-poor blood bound for the right auricle. Inside the device, the blood would be exposed to fresh oxygen, then pumped back into the real heart's left side, which would send it back to the body. It took Sewell several months to finish his project. When it was done, the "heart" looked for all the world like a contraption from an Erector manual. Framed by foot-long perforated plates and braced by girders, the device held valves that were opened and shut by rubber flaps made from a party noisemaker. Various cams and levers on an Erector axle regulated the heart's "beat." And bolted to the box was a 110-volt Erector motor to power the pumping action. Do I have any volunteers for this amazing new surgical technique?

Three dogs were enlisted to test the Erector heart. Anesthetized, cut open, and hooked to the machine, the first was kept alive for sixty-three minutes. As the right side of the dog's heart lay dormant, Sewell's Erector pump worked perfectly, receiving blood, refreshing it, returning it to the body. A few weeks later, another dog's heart was bypassed for 105 minutes. Both animals made full recoveries. The third dog suffered a heart attack when the system's artificial respirator—not built from Erector parts—malfunctioned. The following year, when he graduated from Yale, Sewell reported his findings in the journal *Surgery*. In 1963 Dr. Michael DeBakey performed the first open heart surgery using a pump similar to Sewell's, though not made from an Erector set.

Sewell's Erector heart made the difference between life and death, but most sets made more modest prototypes. Among them:

• In 1940, with England plunged into World War II, Donald Bailey of Britain's Royal Engineers saw the need for a light, portable bridge to help troops span creeks and rivers. Bailey turned to his Erector set. The result was the Bailey Bridge, which, soldiers often joked, looked just like a big Erector model. Advancing Allied troops bolted together hundreds of Bailey Bridges spanning nearly 200 miles of gaps. Along with radar and heavy bombers, General Dwight Eisenhower called the Bailey Bridge one of the three most important technological advancements of the war.

• In 1950, when Bob Fye got a job at General Motors, he didn't forget the toy that had made him an engineer. Nearly a half century after the first automobiles rolled off an assembly line, GM was still molding pistons by hand. Men in asbestos suits sweltered over vats of molten metal, ladling aluminum into cylindrical casts. No matter how carefully they poured, 10 percent of the pistons had to be scrapped. GM asked Fye to design a machine that would cast pistons. After visiting several plants to see how it was done by hand, Fye got out his Erector set. Two twelve-inch girders provided the crossbars. A horizontal girder connected them at each end. Brass pulleys linked by axles made a rolling trolley run along the top of the structure. Gears, levers, and strings raised and lowered tiny buckets to measure exactly enough molten metal to fill the mold. Fye took his prototype to GM. After some jury-rigging, it seemed good enough to mock up. Within a few years, all GM pistons were poured by machine, cutting the reject rate from 10 percent to 2 percent. GM got the patent; Fye got a dollar. He retired from GM in 1976 and now spends much of his time building incredible Erector models he sometimes displays at the Jackson County Fair in Indiana.

• The 100 million people who wear soft contact lenses also owe something to the Erector set. In 1961 Dr. Otto Wichterle, a chemist in Czechoslovakia, was experimenting with a new polymer that could absorb small amounts of liquid. Realizing the polymer might be made into a less irritating contact lens, Wichterle began searching for a way to spin it into small circles. He finally perfected the process—the same one still used for today's soft contacts—using an old phonograph and an Erector set.

These days, it seems that every industry is digitized, its high-tech heightened far beyond the reach of Gilbert's toy. Yet so long as aging engineers remember Erector, its influence will continue. The latest application can be seen at California Adventure, the newest Disney theme park in Anaheim, California. Among the park's most popular attractions is Soarin' Over California. Each morning, visitors line up early to get the feeling of flying. Once past the turnstile, they take seats in three rows, which are then lifted into place directly above an eighty-foot screen. Within seconds, they are flying—virtually, that is. As breezes blow beneath their dangling feet, their seats bank and shift, causing them to "soar" over California's coast, its farmlands, its purple mountains' majesty. Soarin' Over California is the latest in virtual reality. Riders even smell the sea, the flowers, the fields they are supposedly soaring over. Yet the entire attraction would have stayed on the drawing board had Disney Imagineer Mark Summers thrown away his Erector set.

While building his own career, Summers moved thirteen times in eighteen years. Each time he carefully packed his 1962 Cape Canaveral Erector set, the one he had played with daily while growing up in the California desert. He occasionally showed it to his two sons and daughter, but they preferred Legos. Still, he could not throw it away. "It was the only toy I kept," he said. "There was just something about it, something really cool about those gears and levers and bolts." After working for large engineering firms, Summers soon specialized in amusement park rides. He began consulting for Disney, working on Space Mountain, Pirates of the Caribbean, and Maelstrom at Epcot. In 1991 he became a full-time Imagineer and principal engineer for Disney's most high-tech amusements. He took ample advantage of CAD/CAM systems using the latest 3-D modeling software, but then he encountered a problem that could not be solved on-screen.

To make Soarin' Over California really soar, engineers wanted the seats to rise up off the floor, lifting above the screen, hanging in the breeze, tilting with each turn. They considered using a telescoping boom. They pondered rows of seats on sweeping beams. Each seemed too cumbersome, too labor-intensive. Come Thanksgiving weekend in 1996, Summers and his team of engineers were stumped. "The likelihood that this attraction would be built literally rested on finding an efficient way to load guests and move them into the defined viewing positions," he remembered. On Sunday afternoon, while other engineers were watching football, Summers had an idea. What if? He quickly sketched a diagram but knew it would be hard to explain without a model. Then he remembered his Erector set, dusty and neglected, stored in the attic above his garage.

Working into the evening, Summers bolted together a box-like frame, then suspended pulleys and wheels from it. Below he hung three "seats" made from four-inch girders. He topped them with cardboard canopies made from toilet paper tubes. When he turned the crank, the seats moved forward . . . and soared. He put the model in a shopping bag and took it to his meeting the next morning. When he set his model on the table, Summers thought he detected a few smirks from younger engineers. Later he overheard the term "Flintstone engineering." Yet no one could deny that it worked. Could a full-scale version be built, however? A feasibility study suggested that it could, and the model soon made its way through a round of meetings—impressing other engineers, high-level executives, and contractors. In the spring of 2001, when Soarin' Over California opened, passengers soared above the screen thanks to a loading system exactly like the one Summers had built with his Erector set. And the prototype still sits on his desk, when it's not on loan to some other engineer who wants to play with it.

No matter how tightly they cling to their toys, engineers who played with Erector sets are getting older every year. In a decade or two, when all have retired or passed away, where will Gilbert's heritage be preserved? Collectors sell Gilbert memorabilia at their annual conventions and every day on eBay. Log on, type "Erector," and on a typical day, you can choose from more than 200 items peddled by Gilbert enthusiasts. Someone nicknamed "stuffandmorestuff" is selling a 1929 No. 7 Erector set, vintage condition. Two hundred dollars is the top bid. Farther down the list is a No. 7½ set like the one I used to build my Eiffel Tower. Only $84.99. And here's the Young Builder set I got for my eighth birthday. Top bid just $5! But the set hasn't aged well, according to the seller. Its cardboard tube has a burn spot, and what am I to make of the "hole where Dad's face is"? Perhaps I wasn't the only angry young Gilbert boy back in 1961. Bidders on eBay can also buy Gilbert memorabilia, including Mysto magic manuals, Erector parts and motors, empty Erector boxes at a buck apiece, and an old ad that warns "Don't Cheat Your Boy on Christmas Morning!"

Swapping and sharing, some collectors have filled whole basements with Gilbert's toys. Top collectors have one hundred or more Erector sets. Yet curiously, only a handful of Gilbert collectors build with their sets. Most have a working model whirling—a Ferris Wheel or a Carousel—but the sets just sit there opened but untouchable, as if Christmas morning never gave way to Christmas afternoon. To see Gilbert's legacy at play, you have to go to his birthplace, Salem, Oregon.

On the banks of the Willamette River stands a bright yellow three-story Victorian house that once belonged to Gilbert's Uncle Andrew, known in the family as A. T. Gilbert. The home now belongs to children, or at least it's taken over by them every morning. Swarming through the gates, kids celebrate the fun of learning at A. C. Gilbert's Discovery Village. Since 1989, the children's museum has expanded beyond the original Gilbert home. It now includes three old houses moved to the site and a huge backyard playground with a towering climbing sculpture designed to look like an Erector model. The Discovery Village also has Erector sets open for play in one room devoted to Gilbert's life and career.

Kids don't spend much time in the Gilbert room. They prefer bubble displays, dinosaur dioramas, and other exhibits common to children's museums. The Erector sets sit quietly near the displays of Gilbert's science kits, trains, and life story. But each February 15, the village throws its namesake a birthday party. Collectors bring their favorite sets, magicians perform, and kids compete to make the best Erector model. No one wins a car or pony, but a new generation learns how much can be made with just a few girders and some ingenuity.

It's impossible to say what Gilbert would have thought of the museum in his uncle's old home. Would he have understood why it has a model African village or multicultural play structures designed to resemble homes from around the world? Yet it's a safe bet Gilbert would have enjoyed its "good clean fun" and the variety of kids—both boys and girls—playing there. The democracy of the place is embodied in a simple rope trick Gilbert often performed to explain what he was trying to do with his toys. He showed the trick to bankers from whom he sought loans. He performed it for service groups in New Haven and New York. And he did it for his coworkers, probably so often they tired of it. The trick was called the Professor's Nightmare, and Gilbert refused to

include it in his Mysto magic kits, lest he be unable to surprise future audiences.

Standing before each group, Gilbert would take out three
ropes. One was six inches long. This, Gilbert would say, stands
for the youngest boy, about eight years old. The second rope
measured ten inches. This was the older boy, ten to twelve. And
the third was fourteen inches long. This, he would explain to
anyone who didn't get his drift, was the boy thirteen and up. As
he spoke, Gilbert aligned and manipulated the ropes, using hands
that had lost little of their dexterity. Given the "boys'" different
abilities and interests, he asked, how could their needs be met?
He wanted each, regardless of age, to do everything a boy should
do—run, play, build, learn, experiment. Hiding the ropes behind
one palm, keeping their upper ends visible, Gilbert folded them
with his other hand. Finally, he tugged at all three, shook them . . .
and they all came out exactly the same length. Like boys of all
ages growing to be men, he would say, if you just apply a little
magic.

Magic was the key to every toy Gilbert sold. And each
worked a kind of magic back when most Americans made things
instead of just selling them, and when industry, not information,
was the label of the age. Sold separately, each Erector set was
played with until it was scattered, bent, or just abandoned by a
young man with other things on his mind. But collectively, these
Gilbert boys became like the interlocking parts in a single set.
Time assembled them into a nation of tinkerers. For every scientist or engineer among them, there were hundreds who ran a factory machine shop, worked on an assembly line, or repaired
transmissions. Many did little more with their skills than change
the oil in their cars. But together, they built America. They built
the roads, factories, dams, buildings, cars, trucks, and tractors, the
simple gadgets and the rocket science that brought the country
out of the nineteenth century and hurled it toward the twenty-
first. This hand-built nation, despite recent rust, is the same one
we still drive through, fly across in a single day, or put into play

by pushing buttons. It's the techno-country we curse when it breaks down, take for granted when it doesn't, and entrust with our lives every day. Erector sets are antiques now, but the America they inspired their owners to build still goes round and round, and so A. C. Gilbert is still working his magic.

Acknowledgments

Aside from magazine profiles and his autobiography, *The Man Who Lived in Paradise*, not much has been written about A. C. Gilbert. Along with these few public sources, I am therefore indebted to private collectors who continue to cherish Gilbert's legacy. Chief among these are L. Andrew Jugle, whose archive includes whole boxes of old Erector ads, manuals, payrolls, balance sheets, photos, letters, and other material, and Bill Bean, whose complete collection of *Erector Tips* was the source of many stories about Gilbert's childhood and early promotions. I am also grateful to William Massa of Yale's Sterling Memorial Library for access to the three volumes of Gilbert scrapbooks and the Gilbert letters, each lovingly collected by Gilbert's daughter Lucretia. Bill Brown of the Eli Whitney Museum in Hamden, Connecticut, was also generous in opening that museum's archives of Gilbert papers. Thanks also to Gilbert's grandchildren, Jeffrey and Sev Marsted and William Chase, and to his longtime friends and employees Angus Gordon, Herb Pearce, and Charles Ryan, for sharing their memories.

Certain scenes in this book have been embellished by dialogue but are based entirely on research from the above sources.

All stories concerning young owners of Erector sets are based on personal interviews with them or their descendants. Details about the contents of specific Erector sets were obtained from the two-volume *Greenberg's Guide to Gilbert Erector Sets* by William M. Bean and Al M. Sternagle.

Index